Changed Forever

Servant Publications
Ann Arbor, Michigan

Published by Servant Publications
P.O. Box 8617
Ann Arbor, Michigan 48107

Scripture used in the work, unless otherwise indicated, is taken from the New International Version of the Bible, copyright © 1978 by New York International Bible Society, used by permission of Zondervan Bible publishers.

Cover design by Michael Andaloro

92 43 94 95 96 10 9 8 7 6 5 4 3 2 1

Printed in the United States of America
ISBN 0-89283-780-2

Library of Congress Cataloging-in-Publication Data

Changed forever : five stories of God's transforming grace / edited by Robert DeGrandis with Linda Schubert.
     p. cm.
  Includes bibliographical references
  ISBN 0-89283-780-2.
  1. Catholics—Biography. 2. Pentecostalism—Catholic Church.
3. Spiritual life—Catholic authors. 4. Catholic Church—Membership. I. DeGrandis, Robert. II. Schubert, Linda.
BX4651.2.C48   1992
282'.092'2—dc20   91-35749

Other books by
Robert DeGrandis, S.S.J.

The Gift of Miracles
Praying for Miracles
Healing through the Mass
Renewed by the Holy Spirit
Come, Follow Me
Coming to Life
Resting in the Spirit
Healing the Broken Heart
Intergenerational Healing
The Gift of Prophecy
The Gift of Tongues
Layperson's Manual for the Healing Ministry
To Forgive is Divine
The Power of Healing Prayer
The Ten Commandments of Prayer
Introduction to the Catholic Charismatic Renewal
*Healing of Self Image**
*Forgiveness and Inner Healing**

*Coauthored with Betty Tapscott

Contents

Introduction

They overcame him by the blood of the Lamb and by the word of their testimony;... **Revelation 12:11**

"TAKE AND READ," were the words St. Augustine heard, so he opened up the Bible and what he read drew him powerfully toward conversion. St. Ignatius of Loyola, wounded in battle, began to read the lives of the saints. These stories led to the formation of one of the largest religious communities in the church—the society of Jesus, the Jesuits. One priest has said, "If young men would read five powerful Catholic books, such as *Damien the Leper, Our Lady of Fatima, The Way of Divine Love,...* many would receive a religious vocation."

One of the major influences in drawing me toward the priesthood was my fifth-grade teacher, Sr. Regina, a Dominican nun from the Boston, Massachusetts area, who wore a pre-Vatican II white habit. Her deep faith, Irish humor, compassion, and humanness modeled the well-balanced Catholic life. Daily I was impressed by

9

her consistent intention of doing what the Lord was calling her to do. Sr. Regina exemplified the gospel in action.

This same nun was also my teacher in seventh grade—a last-minute change in assignment that was a windfall for me. I enjoyed learning from her in class. As one of her favorites, I wanted to be around Sr. Regina and help clean the room, sweep the floor, and assist in any way she needed help at the end of the day. With her I learned a joy of service that has remained to this day. As an impressionable youngster, my life was deeply influenced by her fully Christian, fully human witness. I thank the Lord for this flesh and blood incarnation of what is best in our faith.

As a priest, the lay evangelist Charlie Osburn has had a deep impact on my outlook. Totally giving of himself with unlimited energy, he has also inflamed the lives of several of my friends who have come under his influence. One of my friends, a local judge, returned from Charlie's school of evangelism with a fresh desire to make Jesus known and loved. My friend's subsequent work in evangelization in a local church impressed me so much that it further influenced my own approach.

In 1981 in a restaurant in Toledo, Ohio, Charlie shared with me his philosophy of never charging for any materials, either books or tapes. He had given away some forty thousand cassette tapes at that time. "You limit the Lord," he said to me. I can still hear those words ringing in my ears. That philosophy is an ideal to which I aspire, although I have never achieved it. Like

Francis of Assisi, Charlie's trust in the Lord goads me to greater sacrifice.

A story in his book, *The Charlie Osburn Story*, has also deeply influenced my understanding of forgiveness. I have traveled around the world, preaching a gospel of love and forgiveness in twenty-eight countries, yet have seldom heard a story of forgiveness that has touched me as deeply as this one. Here are Charlie's own words:

I've come to ask your forgiveness for hating you. Forcing those words out of my mouth was one of the most difficult things I have ever done. They were addressed to my next-door neighbor, whom I hated with a passion for eight years. I would lie awake at night, thinking about ways I could kill him. I fantasized about car bombs, about hiring a hit man from New York, about setting his house on fire in the middle of the night.

The hatred I felt toward this man had contributed to the drinking problem I had developed. The consuming desire for revenge and the drinking resulted in high blood pressure, a hernia, and several other problems. My health was a wreck.

Why did I hate him so much? He had repeatedly molested my son and daughter. My son was eight and my daughter was six when this all started, and it was two years before we discovered it. When we finally did, it was just too much for me. I thought about my little children being stripped of their dignity, and I couldn't stand it. The hatred began to grow.

I was completely serious about killing the man, but I never followed through because I didn't want to go to jail. Only the fear of a prison term kept me from murder. When I finally gave up the idea of killing him, I built an eight-foot fence between his house and ours so that I at least wouldn't have to see him. The sight of him made me sick to my stomach.

Forgive him? How could I? He was sick, but that didn't move me. He had committed an offense against something very precious to me, and I could only react with hatred.

After I committed my life to Jesus, Fr. Jim Smith began to teach me about forgiveness and unconditional love. He showed me the Scriptures that commanded me to love everyone—people who had hurt me as well as people who had been good to me.

"You mean I have to love the man who molested my children?" I asked in disbelief. "Why, he's a horrible human being. He hurt two of God's little children. It's hard enough to think about forgiving him. The idea of loving him makes me ill."[1]

As Fr. Jim kept confronting Charlie with the truth of God's Word—that as we forgive we are forgiven (Mt 6:14-15), about binding and loosing (Mt 18:18), about loving your enemies (Lk 6:27)—he came to know that he simply had no choice. He forgave the man by an act of his will.

When Charlie forgave his neighbor, God took the

next step. About three months later, the man approached Charlie's wife in a supermarket. Pulling out a copy of the New Testament, he told her that he had given his life to Jesus. He had been reconciled with the Catholic church, which he had abandoned years before, and had confessed his sins. He had received God's forgiveness and wanted to thank Charlie and his wife for forgiving him. Three weeks later the man died.

My life has been redirected by the living witness of these two Christians, Sr. Regina and Charlie Osburn—a man and a woman who dared to live the gospel.

God speaks powerfully through testimonies, memorable life experiences which can further produce a great change in others. Everyone loves a good story, especially one that deals with bravery, charity, and personal transformation. Living examples have tremendous power to bring conversion whenever they touch the heart.

As I travel around the world, I hear many priests saying that people are hungry and searching. I believe this is really true. The poet Henry Wadsworth Longfellow said in *A Psalm of Life,* "Life is real, life is earnest, and the grave is not its goal. Dust thou art, to dust returnest, was not spoken of the soul."[2] People today have more leisure time to think about their life, purpose, and lack of peace of mind.

In a survey of retreat houses in the United States the question was asked, "What do people seek most when they come to your retreat house?" The first answer given was "healing." A sick world is seeking healing. The good news of Jesus Christ is a healing gospel.

THE POWER OF TESTIMONIES

People need to read accounts of Christians who have been made whole through the power of Jesus Christ in his Holy Spirit. They need to be reminded that this healing is also available for them. Spiritual, psychological, and physical healing is possible. That is what *Changed Forever* is about.

The following testimonies were gathered to inspire, to encourage, and to motivate the reader to a greater living of the gospel of Jesus Christ, which alone can bring peace to a searching world. Through these accounts of healing of mental illness, difficult relationships with fathers, drug addiction, alcoholism, a degenerating spine, and other physical ills, we find ourselves powerfully reminded of the amazing love of our Lord Jesus Christ.

Most importantly, all of these stories recount how God's grace was transforming, bringing not only immediate physical and emotional healing but ultimately a complete transformation in Christ. Here are powerful stories of brothers and sisters in Christ who were literally transformed from one degree of glory to another as they responded to God's grace in their lives. God literally made them new creations in his Son.

After you read each of these testimonies, I invite you to enter a time of prayer and refection, using the highlights of each story and the prayer that have been provided at the end of each chapter. Simply let the Lord lead, using these sections as a starting point.

Further, if you belong to a prayer group, a community, or some small sharing group in a parish, I invite you and other members of your group to use this book as a basis for healing and spiritual growth. Group discussion questions for each chapter have been provided in an appendix for just that purpose. Of course, individuals could use these questions as well, but they are primarily designed for group discussion and reflection.

My prayer is that the Lord will use each of these personal accounts to stir up new faith. Do you need a miracle? Do you need to experience God's transforming grace? Is there something missing in your life? What he has done for others he will do for you. My prayer is that all of us will take Jesus Christ more seriously, surrender to his will, and receive the gift he offers.

Come and listen, all you who fear God; let me tell you what he has done for me. **Ps 66:16**

---

1. Charlie Osburn with Fred Lilly, *The Charlie Osburn Story* (Pensacola, Florida: Good News Ministries, 1986), pp. 85-88.
2. Henry Wadsworth Longfellow, "A Psalm of Life" (1839) from *The Treasury of American Poetry: A Collection of the Finest by American Poets*, Introduction by Nancy Sullivan (Garden City, New Jersey: Doubleday & Co., 1978), p. 94.

1

Because of the Lord's great love
we are not consumed,
for his compassions never fail.
They are new every morning;
great is your faithfulness.

Lamentations 3:22-23

I'm Not Afraid of the Morning Anymore

Mary Ann Cortes

A native of Nicaragua, Mary Ann Cortes is active in the charismatic renewal in New Orleans, Louisiana. Her miraculous recovery from more than seventeen years of mental illness has been an encouragement to hundreds of people suffering from similar disorders.

BEFORE I BEGIN my testimony I must say that throughout my anguish my mother prayed and prayed and prayed for a miracle. If she were living today she would be proud that her grown daughter is not afraid of the morning anymore.

I was born in Managua, Nicaragua, where my family owned a coffee farm, and was raised in Costa Rica. In a country where people live a very socially active life from infancy, my mental illness did not become appar-

'ent until my pre-teen years. Then it became obvious that I preferred the security of my room to the birthday parties, swimming, music, and movies sought after by most girls my age.

When my parents were divorced I was devastated. The meager feelings of life in me were nearly destroyed at that time. Mother was my life. People used to say I was much too attached to her. After the divorce I felt dead and alone.

Not long after the divorce my mother suffered a massive stroke. I found her on the floor and couldn't understand what had happened. I kept crying out, "Mom, what's the matter?" All she could do was mumble. She couldn't talk. In the ambulance I kept asking the attendant, "What's wrong with her?" He said he didn't know. At the hospital I was kept away from her room and didn't know where they had put her. I raced wildly from room to room and eventually found her surrounded by doctors. They ordered me out of the room and called my uncle to take me home.

I tried to sleep on Uncle Oscar's couch but was too emotionally paralyzed. That's when I first developed insomnia. My mother was in the hospital for a month, initially unable to speak. Once I climbed onto her bed and shook her arm, trying to make her move. "Mom," I cried, "please live. You can't die and leave me. Don't leave me." One day we felt a glimmer of hope when she finally moved a finger. My father and uncle returned and arranged for her to receive physical therapy.

In the coming months my mother went through severe mood changes. In moments of extreme depression she would lash out at me and say, "Why did you let me live? Why didn't you let me die?" Sometimes she would push me away and say, "I don't love you. It's all your fault. I'd be better off dead." When I would comb her hair she would undo it. When I would fix her nails she would deliberately ruin them. Then she began to improve. Although I still loved her, I wondered if I could ever forgive her for the rejection.

TORMENTED BY IMAGINARY SNAKES

The situation became worse when we went into the country to stay on a farm for the summer. I developed an irrational fear of snakes and the sound of opening and closing doors. I became fearful of isolation, of being in unprotected open spaces. I would lock myself in the bathroom and stay there for hours, sitting on the floor or on the toilet seat that I kept closed for fear of snakes and slugs coming up through the plumbing. I was petrified of everything, and wanted to kill myself. Mom was too sick to realize my state of mind.

My mother eventually recovered, a miracle in itself. I became progressively worse, to the point where it became apparent that she couldn't take care of me. My two brothers, my sister, and I were sent to a boarding school. This meant leaving Mother and the haven of my room, which terrified me. The boys moved to the United States and my sister and I went to Nicaragua.

In the Managua airport enroute to school, my

mother turned us over to our aunt and walked away. When my hand was forced out of Mother's, I screamed with horror and became vocally paralyzed. From that moment on I hated my mother, I hated God, the church, and everything else. I hated life.

During the first year of school I could hardly talk. Half alive, I just blindly went through the motions. I was like a walking robot. I felt nothing vibrant in me—no muscles, tissue, or heart—just pain. When I did sleep I would dream of nuns chasing me. I would walk to class with my hands covering my face and keep my face covered in class. The only nun I would respond to in class was the one who allowed me to keep my face covered. I hoped that they would put me in a small locker and let me press buttons to give answers to the teacher. I felt secure in a small, enclosed space where I didn't have to fear anything getting to me.

I hated being pretty. Mom said that being pretty was a curse, that pretty girls suffer. One of my nicknames was "China Doll." The nuns said if we looked in a mirror too much we would see the devil because vanity was a sin. So I would put the mirror down quickly and hide my face.

Then I stopped eating. I would see worms in the cheese, spit out the food, and throw the dish on the floor. The nuns assured me there were no worms in the food, but I refused to believe them. They began sending me special plates of food from their private quarters.

Once when my mother came to visit I totally forgot that she had even been sick. When I greeted her I said in surprise, "Mom, you look so different." She responded, "But I'm not really different." I said, "You look so disfigured." The nuns rebuked me, saying, "Don't tell her she's disfigured, tell her she's beautiful." I said, "I can't tell her she's beautiful—she's ugly." I told my mother I hated her, and I hit her. When she left I ran into church and said, "Lord help me. Take me to heaven now." My emotions were so mixed up, I didn't know if I loved Mother or hated her.

I hated the sunrise; it meant I would have to pretend I was alive for another day. When summer came and I was home with my mother, I would withdraw even more. I hated her—for getting sick, for separating me from my brothers, for my emptiness.

A PSYCHIATRIC ODYSSEY

Upon the advice of the nuns who reported my increasingly antisocial behavior, Mother took me to the Oschner Clinic in New Orleans for psychiatric evaluation. At the age of fifteen, I then began a seventeen-year odyssey of intensive psychiatric care. I was in and out of every mental hospital in the region (except a state charity hospital) and given every type of treatment possible, except electric shock which my mother would not allow. I was diagnosed as an incurable, suicidal, chronic depressive. According to the doctors I would be that way for the rest of my life.

Carefully hoarding my sleeping medicine, antidepressants, and tranquilizers, I planned a fourth suicide attempt. I was determined to take my life but was found unconscious and rushed to the hospital. My body was blue and my mouth was foaming as a priest gave me the last rites. The doctor in charge asked my father, "What did you do to her? She doesn't want to live; we are losing her." Though I began to respond on the fourth day, the doctor told my family that I probably would be a vegetable for the rest of my life.

As my normal body functions returned I looked out at the world with bitter, sad, empty eyes. Four psychiatrists rediagnosed me as a classic manic suicidal depressive, and prescribed high doses of lithium. The other medicines I took during my hospital stays included Stellazine, Thorazine, Melorel, Ativan, Xanax, Dalmane, Tofanil, and Klompin.

While I was beginning to respond to the treatment, my brother Bobby was killed in Vietnam. Because we were so close, I was deeply devastated. Again my life was blown into pieces. The pain was so great I couldn't even cry. I was beyond pain, for myself and for my family. It wasn't fair. I wanted to die and Bobby wanted to live. Why hadn't God taken me instead of my brother?

After another long stay in the hospital I began to respond again and became able to work. Oddly enough, I worked for some doctors who didn't know my psychiatric history, and even excelled in my position. Then my biggest breakdown came following the breakup of a romance with a Jewish man. This time I pleaded with my mother to keep me at home without calling the doctor. She gave in when I promised to take my medicine, and for a short while I appeared to be doing okay.

Most of my family didn't know about my terrible hallucinations, often with snakes and other horrible things. I remember Mother would have to check around and under my bed because I had sensations that snakes were all over me. I told the doctor that I couldn't sleep because I saw the world covered with snake skins. I wouldn't take a bath for fear of snakes, snails, and slugs coming up through the plumbing. Often Mother would have to help me get out of bed because I would see pools of snakes on the floor. She would walk around and say, "See, Mary Ann, there isn't anything here." During meals I would have to eat light-colored food. I was afraid of anything dark because I would see snails and worms in it.

Mother had a large, beautiful balcony filled with all kinds of plants that I tended for a period of time. One evening I saw horrible worms and snails all over the plants and on the ground and all over me. I could even hear them buzzing. I started screaming hysterically, paralyzed with fear. Mother half-carried me inside, holding me until I calmed down and reassuring me that there was nothing on the plants or on me.

I had a fetish for nightgowns. One night when I was hallucinating I grabbed all my nightgowns and cut them into pieces. Laughing and crying hysterically I threw the pieces all over the room. Mother ran into my room and tried to stop me. After hours of struggling, I eventually took some medication and calmed down.

The following morning my doctor called and asked to see me. Not remembering the events of the previous night, I obediently went to his office. I was immediately admitted to the hospital and placed in restraints. Later I found out that both my mother and father had called the doctor. This was another long-term stay.

After my discharge my mother took the advice of my doctor and went to Nicaragua to tend our coffee farm. Depressed and furious with her for leaving, I slept twenty-four hours a day, getting up only to shower and eat. No one ever seemed to understand that I just didn't want to live.

While she was in Nicaragua my mother died of a stroke. I was twenty-five years old and unable to handle another stress in my life. Holing up in my father's vacant condominium in Slidell, Louisiana, I became an angry recluse. I kept the drapes closed, disconnected the phone, and slept all the time. When my father came to check on me one day he found me hiding in a closet.

GOD'S MESSENGERS

Again I returned to the hospital. During that period I befriended a teenager who was in the hospital because of drug addiction. Something about his deep pain got through to me; I wanted to help him. After my discharge I was flipping through the television channels one day and saw Danny Abramowitz, a former New Orleans football player, being interviewed by a nun. I later discovered the program was Mother Angelica's. When Danny spoke of working with alcohol and drug abusers I thought of my friend in the hospital.

Somehow I found the Center for Jesus the Lord, the charismatic renewal center in New Orleans. When Sr. Olga answered the phone I explained I was seeking Danny Abramowitz to help a friend on cocaine. She replied that he was not there. Sensing my personal despair, Sr. Olga invited me to attend a service at the Center the following day.

When I opened the door to the Center I thought it was the wrong door. How wrong I was. For the first time I had opened the right door! The usher took me to the front pew. I later learned that it was a retreat and healing service. Sitting there in wonderment I noticed a priest staring at me. It made me feel uncomfortable. Outwardly I was sitting down but inwardly I wanted to curl up in a fetal position.

After the service I met Sr. Olga, who took me to see Fr. Emile Lafranz. Shortly after being with him he heard my confession and reassured me that Jesus loved me. I looked at him in disbelief and said, "Jesus loves me?" "Yes," he repeated, and encouraged me to return to the Center the following Sunday.

During Mass the following Sunday I noticed the priest who had been gazing at me so intensely the previous week. After the final blessing I ran into the sacristy to meet him, not knowing who he was. I learned that he was Fr. Robert DeGrandis. I was amazed at how much he seemed to intuitively know about me. At his request I agreed to go to a Life in the Spirit Seminar, without knowing its purpose. Nothing much seemed to happen at the seminar; I didn't feel any different. Yet I knew inside that something had changed.

The next time I saw Fr. DeGrandis he invited me to a healing service. As Father was praying over a lady during the service, I suddenly realized I could no longer see him. I had been transported into a heavenly realm. I heard beautiful music; I saw a big white cloud and an angel. I was so overwhelmed with joy and love and song that something came bubbling up from deep inside. I was praying in the Spirit.

When I left the service Fr. DeGrandis handed me a copy of the "Forgiveness Prayer" and told me to say it for thirty days. I began to feel better and better. While these spiritual experiences were going on I canceled appointments with my doctor who had strongly advised me to stay away from church. A priest I had spoken to earlier in connection with my friend on cocaine had also advised me to stay away from the charismatic renewal. He said the emotional nature of the renewal could be detrimental to my stability. I didn't listen to either of them.

Because I had canceled several appointments, the doctor called my father and told him I was beginning to withdraw again. In the past my withdrawal had always preceded a period of hospitalization. My father ordered me back to therapy, unwilling to believe my new inner strength was real and lasting. I told the doctor I was going through inner healing and attending church and that I was all right.

After six months of inner healing I went to my doctor again and insisted, "You must listen to me for a change." I told him about inner healing and that I hadn't cried for months; I told him that I wanted to live as I was not afraid of the morning anymore. He still refused to take me off medication, convinced that this was just another manic stage.

Fr. DeGrandis sent me to see Elizabeth Sheldon for deeper inner healing. I went to prayer meetings, praise rallies, conferences, and daily Mass. My whole life had changed. After I heard Fr. DeGrandis' teaching on the Eucharist, I regularly turned to Mass as a source of on-going healing. I became more and more alive. I was in love with Jesus, in love with the Center of Jesus the Lord, with people, with the whole world. I was high all right—but not manic.

After a year my doctor took me off several medications and told me to report back periodically. He said he didn't understand what I was doing and didn't really believe in it, but had to admit that I was different. "Continue what you are doing," he smiled. "I see life in you." As I floated out of his office I said, "I feel like the bride of Jesus." He smiled and responded, "I'll be here if you need me." That was in 1986.

I became actively involved with volunteer work in the community, at the Center, and for Fr. DeGrandis. My family was amazed, hesitant but pleased. They finally began to believe God's healing work in my life after a near fatal automobile accident in which I severely injured my back and legs. Secure and safe in Jesus during the recovery period, I still did not suffer mental regression.

A SURPRISE REUNION

When I was on a retreat in Birmingham, Alabama, Fr. DeGrandis asked me to share my personal testimony on the opening night. A loving, beautiful woman named Kathy was especially drawn to me. I felt a bond with her also; we spent time together, talking and praying. Saturday evening when the conference was over, I was working at the book table when she came up and began to talk with me.

Kathy said that my testimony had touched her very deeply, then asked if I had ever been a patient at De-Paul Hospital in New Orleans. Surprised, I answered that I had been there for a time. Kathy responded, "Mary Ann, I remember you. When you spoke about walking around with your face covered you looked so familiar to me. It didn't hit me until later. Do you remember me? When I was in training on the unit a nurse told me that yours was one of the worst cases of depression that I would ever encounter."

Kathy described how she was assigned the job of escorting me from the unit to the dining area. She would come and get me out of my chair and hold onto my hand. Once when she let go of my hand to get other patients, I got away from her. The other patients called out, "Mary Ann's in her room again... Mary Ann's in her room again... Mary Ann's in her room again." She said when she went back to get me I was all curled up with my face covered.

Kathy said she remembered me very clearly, but was in disbelief that I would be where I am today. She later testified about her earlier experience with me to the other people attending the retreat: "Everyone here is charmed by Mary Ann's personality, yet I remember her when she was sick. The nurses on her unit told me she was one of the worst cases of withdrawal in their experience."

Since that retreat I have received many phone calls and letters. A man on the retreat going through severe depression said he was on many of the medications I had previously taken. He could not believe that I had made it to where I am today. I said, "Doug, there is even more hope for you because you want to get well. I wanted to die."

Recently my father came to my apartment to visit, and we ended up spending the afternoon together. We got my car fixed and just spent time comfortably talking and visiting. I discovered that, perhaps for the first time since I was a small child, Dad was not afraid to be with me. When he asked my opinion about some things, it made me feel worthwhile and valuable. This visit marked a major change in our relationship.

I asked him, "Pappa, was I really that depressed all those years?" Tears came to his eyes as he nodded his head. I said, "Pappa, I gave my testimony in front of thousands of people when I was in California at the convention." He smiled again. "Would you consider me a miracle, Pappa? Did you ever think you would see me like I am today?" He said gently, "You are definitely a miracle, Mary Ann." I said, "Pappa, have you ever seen me this happy?" He said, "You're always happy now." I sighed peacefully. Something deep inside my heart was healed that day as I sat beside my father in my apartment in New Orleans.

❖❖❖

Highlights of Mary Ann's Story

- Reaching out to help a friend on cocaine, Mary Ann receives help from Sr. Olga at the Center for Jesus the Lord.
- She receives the Sacrament of Reconciliation from Fr. Emile Lafranz.
- She attends a Life in the Spirit Seminar.
- She begins to use the forgiveness prayer.
- She receives inner healing.
- She attends praise rallies, prayer meetings, and daily Mass.
- She reaches out to help and pray with others.
- She shares her testimony with others.

Prayer

Lord Jesus, you give us the will to live, the will to choose life, the ability to believe that there is a future and a hope. Through your Holy Spirit, we come to believe that you have good things in store, that you have a wonderful plan and purpose for our lives, that there is meaning and purpose beyond our limited vision.

When you lift the veil of depression, the darkness

goes and the light comes. You are the light of the world. You show us how we are to be a part of your plan of bringing light to a darkened world. I thank you, Lord, that after the healing and transformation, you energize us and move us in a direction that can bring healing and hope to others.

Lord, I thank you that when life and situations look impossible, with no hope for change, your Holy Spirit and power move in and work miracles in our lives that we so desperately cry out to receive. Even when we are not aware of our hearts crying out, you hear the whisper of our hearts, calling out for healing and new hope.

I thank you again, Lord, for the incredible miracle that you have manifested in my life, that tells the world about your love and your care and your mercy. I thank you, Lord, that the new life in me that you have brought about continues to show to the world what is possible to believe for, in the midst of hopeless situations.

I pray now for all those who are oppressed and in the darkness of despair and depression. Lord Jesus, I lift them all up to you and ask you to pour out your Holy Spirit through your merciful heart. Send an angel of mercy to minister to them as you ministered to me. Let them know there is life after depression—that there can be an end to depression. Sweet Jesus, just as you opened the door for me, open the door for my brothers and sisters, that they can see and believe that all things are possible through your divine mercy and love.

Lord, I praise you and thank you for healing me and bringing me up from the depths of despair and emptiness, for keeping me safe in you, for making me a new creation. As you so gently and tenderly touched me, touch all of those who are deeply wounded. I place each of them in your Sacred Heart and cover them with your precious Blood. Lord, have mercy on all in mental hospitals and under psychiatric care. Lord, have mercy. Lord, have mercy. Lord, have mercy.

You are love. You are healing. You are alive in the Eucharist, the miracle medicine for broken and destroyed persons. Lord, I bow before you and thank you for blessing each of these people now. In Jesus' name I pray. Amen.

2

Therefore, if anyone is in Christ,
he is a new creation;
the old has gone, the new has come!
All this is from God, who reconciled us to
himself and gave us
the ministry of reconciliation:
that God was reconciling the world
to himself in Christ,
not counting men's sins against them.
And he has committed to us
the message of reconciliation.

2 Corinthians 5:17-19

TWO

Gently Flows the Dawn

Brenda M. Walsh

Brendan Walsh is a full-time Catholic evangelist residing in Tralee, County Kerry, Ireland, with his wife Geraldine and five children. His life had numerous strikes against it, including childhood abuse, deprivation, drug addiction, epilepsy, and brain damage. The medical profession was ready to put him in an institution to die, but God had another plan. Brendan's story will open your heart to God's amazing grace and stir up new faith in his power to turn around the most impossible circumstances.

M Y STORY IS A TESTIMONY of God's mercy and his desire to bring everyone to salvation. His love brought me to a place of decision and healing, after twenty-five years of darkness and self-destruction. I especially want to thank Mary, our Blessed Mother, for leading me to the feet of Jesus. I ask for her intercession for all who read this. May Jesus grant you hope, healing, peace, and love through your reconciliation to God.

Ireland is a beautiful land. Kerry, the county of my birth, lies at the southwestern tip of Ireland. From the sixth-century Christian chapel on the Dingle peninsula to the roaring thunder of the North Atlantic Ocean, Ireland's rugged beauty inspires the most noble thoughts in those who are in tune with nature. One cannot escape a sense of timelessness here as the Atlantic wind whistles tentatively through the weatherbeaten trees and misty valleys spotted with little fresh water lakes. For thousands of years it has done the same, reminding each generation of how quickly life passes.

Tralee is the largest town in Kerry. Its people, like all those in Ireland, have suffered great oppression through the centuries until relatively recent times. Oppression, however, breeds virtue, with wit and humor as allies. In the early fifties this was evident when mass emigration once again took so many from our shores in search of work. Employment was scarce, but even in the midst of poverty could be seen a close and vibrant community spirit.

I was born into such a community in 1954. The second youngest of seven children, I was proudly named Brendan Marian because my birthday was near the feast of St. Brendan in a Marian year. My earliest childhood memories were sweet and serene. Sitting on the pavement outside our house, I could hear the musical ba-ba-baluba of my older brother John and his makeshift band that included a homemade bass accompanied by washboards and scrub brushes. While

John and his band were popular with the neighborhood children, I was more preoccupied with the little crawling creatures who were unfortunate enough to cross my path.

All our neighbors had large families that roamed freely in and out of each other's homes. Keys were always left in the doors, even at night when everyone was in bed. Poverty brought its own blessings, along with a common bond of concern. As a family we were lucky. Though the wages were low, at least my father had work. There was happiness in that little neighborhood and a sparkle in the eyes of its people.

My family had a curious mixture of characters—from John's rock and roll, my sister Maura's talents in singing old Irish songs, to the various gifts of my other brothers and sisters. My father was an ex-boxer, intelligent and witty with little trace of emotion. Mother, on the other hand, was a petite, black-haired bundle of fun. She poured love upon her children and charmed everyone with her lively personality and sweet smile.

Everything changed in 1959 when my mother became ill and died of cancer, just five days before my fifth birthday. When my father heard the news he fled to a shed behind the house and screamed and cried mournfully.

In those days there were no funeral parlors in Ireland. The body of the deceased was kept in the home overnight until the following evening when it would be carried to the local church. I shall never forget the morning my mother died. Having no concept of the meaning of death, I strolled alone into the room where she lay covered with a white sheet. Beside her bed on a table stood two lighted candles, a crucifix, and some holy water. A strong smell of disinfectant filled the darkened room. From the kitchen I could hear the muffled voices of those gathered to pay their respects.

I tried to speak to Mother but there was no reply. Her normally active hands were white and still, clutching her familiar rosary beads. Confused, I continued to try and wake her, but was soon discovered and carried from the room.

The activity continued the following day as neighbors and friends constantly came by to pay their respects. I paid little heed to the stories, the respectful laughs, and the tears. As long as my mother's body remained in the bedroom I didn't care what else happened. In the evening her body was surrounded by people praying the sorrowful mysteries of the rosary. When the rosary was finished and the people had gone, two strangers came and twisted the screws on the coffin lid.

For the first time the shocking reality pierced my little heart. I would never see my mother's face or hear her voice again. Fate had dealt a cruel blow.

As the months passed my father became more and more introverted and bitter, turning over responsibility for household chores to my older sister, Maura, who was then seventeen. Without notice he would often fly into a blind rage, using all kinds of verbal abuse. We were all frightened of him.

Father quickly severed our friendship with close relatives and began to inflict a cruel discipline on all the children. We became for him objects of contempt, reminders of a life that no longer existed. There was no more music and laughter in the home. The joy and imagination that flow out of security and a sense of well-being were now gone. The key was taken from the door, neighbors were no longer welcome, and our once vibrant home became a place of isolation.

Through the early years there endured in each of us an overwhelming desire to please our father. We competed for his love but always fell short, and ended up being rebuffed and ridiculed. Just as the mother we knew and loved had died, so too, in some strange way, had our father. The love of a child is difficult to kill, however. When my father was away I would lie awake in my bed at night and stare nervously at the ceiling. Wondering where he was, I would cry and imagine he would never come home. How relieved I would feel when I would hear the front door opening. Just to know he was safe was like a sedative. Sleep quickly followed.

During a period of five years we moved twice. Maura and John left to live with relatives, then my sisters Saora, Naomh, and Orla were taken by my grand aunt. Shane and I remained at home. My father was angry with what he termed as the desertion of my brother and sisters and swore that they would never again darken the door to his house.

Though two years older than I, Shane found it difficult to take a beating. One Christmas, we were instructed to box each other with our gift of new boxing gloves. We fought ferociously, trying desperately to impress our father. The fight was bloody and hard, but according to him neither of us won. Father then began to instruct us on how to box properly. His punches were too hard, but we could only take the punishment and hope that he would soon realize he had gone too far. Often his lips would be tight and his eyes dark with anger but we didn't dare protest. That would have made the situation worse.

Beatings and intimidation continued to be a regular occurrence. Sometimes I admitted to things my brother had done because I knew he was unable to take the pain. Shane eventually withdrew and suppressed his emotions, but I grew hard. I somehow resolved to take all my father could dish out. To him that meant defiance, so he did everything he could to break me. Often he split my skin and once left me unconscious.

I became even more difficult and defiant to the point where most of the punishment was deserved. At school where corporal punishment was still enforced, I was always doing something to warrant the blows. I took my frequent punishment with contempt while secretly planning some future resistance. I was filled with defiance and developed a deep desire to hurt others. As long as I hurt them first, they could not hurt me. I could not betray my father's violence—both from pride and fear of the consequences. My role was set. My image was created. Hardness became for me a way to survive.

Though our lives were set in misery, my brother and I found ways to laugh. We had a terrific sense of humor, made jokes, wrestled, and had fun. I honestly believe that it was this humor, balanced against the pain of rejection, that helped us to survive those years. We would dream of better times and make extravagant plans for our future. Other times we would laugh hysterically for hours at a time, imitating the different expressions of our father in his anger.

ADRIFT WITHOUT AN ANCHOR

We were a Catholic family, but apart from the catechism taught at school we had no religious upbringing. There was no prayer in the home, no talk of God. We were under the impression that we were masters of our own destiny—a very frightening and desperate challenge. With no highly developed sense of morality, nobody mattered but me. At the age of thirteen I also found myself in the midst of a changing Irish society where the rigid moral fabric was beginning to deteriorate. It was a time to explore and exploit, to exert power over others.

I was attracted to girls but never wanted to admit it. In that thirteenth year I met Clare, an extraordinary and beautiful girl who was two years older and also reaching out for affection. Hers was the first gentle touch in my life since the death of my mother. After a year of wonderful intimacy, Clare left Ireland to join relatives abroad. The memory of our time together was the most positive thing that had happened to me. Somebody actually loved me. I didn't have to protect myself or frighten her away.

After Clare was gone, my friends and I would roam the town at night looking for action. When we couldn't find any, we made it ourselves. We were cheeky, smart, and sarcastic, always wanting to create some excitement. One evening I was approached by the manager of a cafe who was aware of my rebellious behavior. A stranger in town, he took particular interest in me and encouraged my rebellion, defining it as courageous and legitimate.

As our friendship grew my new friend took me to a country house and introduced me to some of his companions, a strange mixture of long-haired men and women. He also introduced me to hashish. The group welcomed me and seemed genuine in their acceptance of me. They were gentle and funny, expressing opinions on just about everything. They sensed my hurt and tension and encouraged me to freely express my feelings through the shared use of drugs.

During some of those supposedly therapeutic sessions, women would take me to their bedrooms. For a kid who had no sense of morality, I felt I had discovered paradise. Eventually bored with hashish, L.S.D. introduced me to a whole new world—a world without dimensions, a mixture of color and light and often terror and darkness. In the midst of the rock music, drugs, and incense, our group talked of going to Brazil to escape the disturbed and inhibited society. We felt the need to return to nature, to be at one with it, to be free and impulsive.

By this time my father spent more time out of the house, and my brother had left to study management training. I was no longer afraid of my father's temper. I had already weathered too many insults and degrading remarks, too many blows, too many winter nights sleeping in closet-type sheds or in the back of parked trucks. Now and then I would return home to offset any inquiry or suspicion. My school saw little of me as well.

I felt I was shaking loose from the oppression and a disgusting mundane existence and that I was supported by true friends, people who cared, people who were gentle and intelligent. But in time my newfound friends grew restless and one by one began to drift away. Soon I was alone again, in a town that I now saw as antiquated and inhibiting. So at the age of fifteen I packed my bags and left for London. Upon my arrival I think I must have tried to say "Hello" to just about everyone that passed by, as was the custom in my home town. I soon learned, however, that in this place one had to avoid such niceties.

It wasn't difficult finding a job. I lied about my age and was given employment in a Jewish firm that made detergents and rat poison. I soon made new friends and was into drugs again, living in a world of dimly lit basements and all-night parties. I began to suffer from memory loss and physical weakness. London, though a vibrant city, became for me the loneliest place in the world.

Tired and frightened, I returned to Ireland and continued using drugs. Sometimes when I looked in the mirror my face would feel like it was splitting in two. Once while out walking I looked down to see thousands of imaginary spiders crawling up one side of my body and onto my face where they seemed to be devouring my flesh.

When my drug activities were eventually reported, the police gave me the choice of being prosecuted or undergoing voluntary treatment. I opted for treatment. My time in the hospital left me in a deep depression. Although I was just sixteen years of age, my hair was turning grey and I felt like an old man. Even worse, I had lost my most valuable asset—my Irish sense of humor.

For almost a year following my release from the hospital, I remained silent and still. Separated from life, I was on the outside looking in. I felt no desire to live or to die. I didn't even feel pain. I felt nothing.

GOD'S GENTLE HAND

God's providence is most remarkable. He has a way of working in our lives even when we are unable to recognize his existence. There are virtually thousands of times in a person's life when God's gentle hand leads and encourages without ever infringing on dignity or free will. This was certainly the case when, after my seventeenth birthday, my father asked me if I would join the army. Knowing I was an embarrassment to him and to myself, I agreed. God's gentle, guiding hand was at work.

On March 6, 1972, I left for enlistment. There was sleet on the ground as I walked through the security gate at the military barracks. I was given all kinds of tests along with the others who were also enlisting. The medical examination was crude and embarrassing, as we stood there practically naked in the biting cold amid muffled sounds of laughter. I was amazed when they told me I had passed. Within twenty-four hours my long-haired companions and I were transported to a military training center. We later discovered our destination had a national reputation for scrupulous attention to the formation of soldiers.

The new enlistees were billeted in the same block and were soon marched awkwardly to the barber shop. The scene was hilarious. With hysterical laughter and tears, we watched our long hair dropping to the floor like wool being shorn from sheep. The barber had a fixed smile on his face as he freely expressed his art.

It wasn't long before we received uniforms and weapons. The sergeant major informed us that we were now the property of the state. He promised us solemnly that he would fashion our characters and our bodies into suitable instruments—regardless of how horrible, ugly, or feebleminded we might be.

The sergeant major was true to his promise. We went through the most rigorous training. Even a cold look toward a superior officer guaranteed a charge of presumption. Every moment was structured and disciplined. The daily drills and routines developed in me a new determination. This was the very therapy I needed to pull me out of my stupor. Before long I was alive, vibrant, fit, and alert.

During my time off I met Geraldine, a fiery sixteen-year-old who was to become the greatest single influence in my life. Her father was dead and her mother had left home when she was a little girl, so Geraldine was raised by her grandfather. At first she resisted all my advances and didn't think twice of using her fists to put me in my place.

Eventually though, Geraldine came to love me. And it wasn't long before she became pregnant. When we were at a Count Dracula movie and he was about to bite his victim's neck, Geraldine told me the news. We decided to get married—against the advice of a priest who predicted that the marriage would not last a year. My response to him was, "Sure, a year is an awfully long time, Father."

Not many months later our daughter Jacqueline was born. The nurse at the hospital counted all her toes and fingers and assured me that my daughter was perfectly formed. Geraldine and I were both proud to have Jacqueline; to this very day she has blessed our lives by her presence.

In the fall of 1973, I was chosen to travel to the Middle East with a United Nations Peace Keeping Force of one hundred and fifty men. I had worked hard during the training period. Since I wasn't tall I knew I had to be the best. It was a great honor and a sign of recognition to be chosen from a pool of thousands of men all over Ireland. During my seven-month tour of duty between Cairo and the Sinai Desert, I became aware of the smell and sounds of death. The whistling of bullets left my companions and me fully aware that life was on borrowed time.

Following that exciting assignment, I considered the

advice of an officer and decided to enter cadet school. I had finally discovered my calling in life. I was fit, healthy, and confident. The world was my oyster. Little did I know what tomorrow would bring.

One morning after returning from a run, I blacked out. After regaining consciousness I felt weak and tired, with blood coming from my mouth. Thinking my illness was stress-related, I went on a regimen of vitamins. When the blackouts continued, a series of tests taken at the military hospital in Cork resulted in a diagnosis of grand mal epilepsy. The doctors advised me that this condition would remain with me for the rest of my life. At the age of twenty, my world caved in again.

All my old hatreds and bitterness returned. I rejected everything and everyone, including my wife and child. I began drinking and running around with women, wanting to hurt everyone in my path. I was filled with destruction. Having been discharged from the army, I couldn't believe all my efforts had been wasted. I felt vulnerable and somehow undermined. My sense of security was gone and only panic remained.

Geraldine did her best to calm me. We decided to return to my native town of Tralee in County Kerry. Why she remained with me I shall never understand, because I took most of my anger out on her. The very anger and degradation my father had directed toward me I now redirected toward my wife. Geraldine remained patient and gentle with me in spite of my unfaithfulness and rage. We even had another child during this time, a son. I studied accounting and general management during the day, yet when night came

I would revert to my old pattern of women and alcohol. I became a time bomb waiting to explode.

RAVAGED BY ILLNESS

By the winter of 1978 I had regained some status and respect, but inside I felt sick and degraded. Nothing seemed able to make up for what was missing, to fill the emptiness. I disliked myself intensely. During this period I was taking heavy medication for my many seizures and experiencing a diminished capacity to function normally. What previously took hours to do now began to take days.

With everything getting out of control I expected disaster at every step. I seemed to be two people: one trying to become successful and make a lot of money to insulate himself against hurt; the other blindly throwing away his life, empty and broken, lonely and confused. I lived in such fear of the darkness inside that I could no longer resist the temptation to take my own life.

One day when Geraldine and the children were away, I calmly assessed my life. There seemed nothing in it of worth. I felt like a fraud and a coward. I knew that I had neither the courage and determination, nor the ability to make something meaningful out of my life. My conclusion was that the greatest act of kindness to myself and my wife and children would be to die.

I was completely resigned to this decision. God never entered my thoughts. The idea of everlasting sleep filled me with peace: no more struggle, pain, hurt, or fear and no shadows of the past to haunt me. I was ready and even longed for the finality of death. I got out my tablets (Phenobarbitone, Epenutin, and Librium), swallowed as many as I could, then lay down on the bed to die. But even then God's providential hand was near.

Our apartment manager's son, a psychiatric nurse, was home from London on a visit and wanted to see me. The apartment manager knew I was home, so when I didn't answer the door he let himself in and found me unconscious. I was rushed to the hospital. My wife was told that the antidote administered probably would be too much for my system and to expect the worst.

Three days later in intensive care when I opened my eyes for the first time, I felt a great sense of shame for having failed in my suicide attempt. The doctor told Geraldine that my brain was damaged and that it would continue to get worse. They stated that my potential for violence would increase to the point that it would not be safe for her or the children to remain with me. They said that within one year I would be institutionalized and advised her to leave me. Geraldine refused to listen and took me home.

By the fall of 1979 I was rapidly deteriorating with increased panic attacks and hallucinations. Word came that my father had died. Standing alone beside his coffin in the funeral parlor, I was filled with sadness. I placed my two arms around his shoulders and hugged him tightly—the only hug I ever remember between my father and me. As my brothers and sisters and I gathered around his grave, we seemed like strangers to each other. It could have been so different.

My memory flashed back to my mother and my dim reflections of the joy and innocence of childhood. I felt a great sorrow as I considered the lost potential. My father was gone but within each of us remained the scars and the hurt. No longer did I have him as a visible target for my anger. He had been wrenched from life without warning, deprived of all possibility of some form of reconciliation with his children. Father did, however, receive the last rites, which I later understood to be an act of God's mercy.

After my brothers and sisters left, life went on as before. I felt curiously alone and free. By now my speech was at times a little slurred, and when I walked I would sometimes trip over myself. One day a woman stopped by and left a rosary. I felt insulted by her insinuation that we needed to pray. As a family we never went to Mass and the thought of praying to a God who was the architect of our misery seemed repulsive and stupid. I felt it was just another offer of a straw to hang onto.

Nonetheless, I began to pray the rosary, asking for Mary's intercession with God, not for the restoration of my health, but for the material wealth that would insulate me against the pain of the world. I felt slightly amused by such a proposal. If God really existed, it seemed to me that he owed me one because of the destruction he had caused. Though my motives were frivolous and wrong, I now believe the prayers were heard by Mary and through her intercession brought to Jesus. In spite of my attitude, change was coming.

By 1980 my family and I had moved to our own little home. One evening a friend invited me to go to a prayer meeting in the local school hall. He had a sense of joy about him and declared confidently that 1980 was going to be a special year for me. I felt somewhat less enthusiastic than my friend, but his power of persuasion was strong. I agreed to go, providing I could sit by the door and leave if I wanted.

On Pentecost Sunday, I dressed and made my way to the school hall. I noticed that the morning was unusually sunny and heard the sweet chirping of the birds. As I entered the hall I was greeted and given a hymn sheet. I placed my chair at the back of the hall beside the door. Before me stood a host of middle-aged women and some men with hands raised in the air, making strange babbling sounds.

Almost immediately I began to feel an oncoming panic as perspiration began to roll down my face and neck. When a man stood up to speak about Jesus I tried to offset my panic by questioning why a layman was speaking of Jesus in a Catholic gathering. As he told of how Jesus suffered and died for each of us, the rhythm of my breathing changed. By now I was taking in great gulps of air and glancing at the door.

Suddenly I sensed that Jesus was a living entity, a reality and not just an historical figure. My panic grew worse. Even my hair became wet with perspiration. My stomach began to cramp and I felt I had to get out of there. When I tried to get up to leave, I felt two hands press lightly on my shoulders. I turned to see who touched me but could see only the wall.

As I faced the front of the hall again I felt a strange peace, my panic subsided, and the perspiration stopped. My whole body felt cool and my breathing returned to normal. From then on I could clearly hear every word that was spoken. Every mention of Jesus made me heavy with the guilt of my offense. I prayed, "God, I am sorry for who I am. I wish I could be someone different, but I cannot change who I am. This is me, and I just can't turn back the clock."

During a break I went to the corridor to smoke a cigarette and noticed a confessional. The desire to go to confession overwhelmed me. I just knew I had to confess my sins. I expected fiery judgment as I laid out my life before the priest, but what I received instead was the compassion of Christ. When I left I felt a peace and lightness I cannot describe. I knew I was forgiven. If that were all I would receive that day it would have been enough. For the first time in my life I felt clean inside. The Holy Spirit had washed my guilty heart in the blood of Jesus.

After I returned to the hall, I was able to cherish every moment of the rest of the meeting. Each word, each prayer, penetrated deeply into my heart. I found it difficult to hold back the tears. When the meeting was over the speaker asked if he could pray with me. I didn't quite understand what he meant by this, so with a little embarrassment I said yes. When this man touched me on the forehead I fell to the floor. The words that came from heaven were like thunder: "I have chosen you; you have not chosen me."

Then in a vision I saw myself looking down as if from a high place at my body on the floor. Beside me knelt a long-haired man in a white robe, visible only from the back as he held one arm under my head. Then the vision changed and I was looking into his face. There were tears flowing from his eyes and I knew it was Jesus. I thought, "The reason he is crying is because I have offended him."

At that moment the thunderous voice came again: "My Son is not crying because he is sad; he cries tears of joy because today you allowed him to snatch you from the pit." Jesus had baptized me in his Holy Spirit. The love of God penetrated every aspect of my being. Pictures began to flow through my mind, incidents of the past which had left me deeply scarred. As each one came, a hand gently pushed it to the side.

For the first time in my life, I felt truly loved. When I stood up from the floor I began to speak in words that were foreign to me. I had received the gift of tongues, the ability to pray in the Spirit.

God can do so much more than we ask or think. I left that meeting a whole person. The Holy Spirit had united me with Jesus and I was healed in my spirit, soul, and body! He restored my dignity and I faced homeward with new purpose and new hope.

In just one instant in time, Jesus had lifted me from the depths of despair and destruction and animated within me a burning desire to reach the ultimate goal of eternal life with him. My life had been beyond all human help, but the love of almighty God reached out and saved me—not because I was worthy but because he loved me.

Nothing can weaken God's love for us. "I love you with an everlasting love," says the Lord. "I am constant in my affection for you." That promise remains for all of us, regardless of how sinful and broken we may be. Jesus lives and is the same yesterday, today, and forever. I can never repay him for his merciful intervention in my life. I can only thank him and say with my limited human understanding, "Jesus, I love you."

What joy was in my heart when I returned home that day. With the greatest sincerity I held Geraldine in my arms and asked her forgiveness. To my children, too, I expressed my sorrow and regret for not being the father I should have been. My past now no longer held me in bondage. Gone were the hatred and bitterness that stole from me the peace, joy, and hope that were always mine in Jesus. The past was gone and only the future remained, a future that I now knew would not stop with my earthly existence but would carry on for all eternity in the company of the object of all my love, Christ Jesus our Lord.

RESTORATION AND RENEWAL

During the following two weeks, I shed many tears of joy. I was able to forgive all who had hurt me, most especially my father. I realized that from an evil situation God can bring forth the greatest good. I can now see the abiding grace of the Holy Spirit from my baptism as a baby. He was able to take all the evil in my life and still create a beautiful life for God. If this is what it took to bring me to the understanding I now have, then it was all worth it. In reflecting back on my suicide attempt, I saw God's mercy and providence in intervening to save my life.

The news of my dramatic conversion brought many invitations to speak. On one such outing the Lord spoke to my heart and told me to return home and teach my family. I pleaded with him to let me continue my speaking engagements, but in my heart I knew he was right. I canceled the other talks and returned home.

During all of the eighties, I invested most of my time and energy in my family. Geraldine experienced a wonderful conversion in 1983 and we had three more children, bringing the total to five, three boys and two girls. As I taught and encouraged my family, I learned so much from them in return. The expression of love from my innocent children reflected in a most profound way the simplicity of God. Their sense of security and well-being, as well as their trust in us as their parents, allowed me to understand the joy of God the Father as he looks down upon his little children.

The hope I held for my children's future allowed me to understand that God sees each of us as we will be in eternity. As we watched and blessed them in their sleep, we caught a glimpse of the protective nature of God the Father. Those years also became a time of intense study as I applied myself to theology and church history, as well as contemporary philosophy. I worked at odd jobs to provide for my wife and children and marveled at how Jesus will go to any lengths to preserve the family.

We all shared a time of being living witnesses to the power of Christ. Hundreds of people have come to a deep personal relationship with Christ while observing our family attempting to live the gospel message. They have come to know that, through the Holy Spirit, Jesus can be their strength and protection as they have observed his care for us. They have come to know that it is the Holy Spirit who fights their battles as they put their trust in Jesus.

In August 1985, a man named Jerry called to see us. He had been the victim of a cruel divorce proceeding in England and had lost his house and most of his possessions and eventually his job as well. He had then returned to Ireland where two years later, unable to find work, he fell into deep depression. Jerry felt empty, rejected, and useless. What bothered him the most was that his eight-year-old daughter had stopped communicating with him.

When Jerry arrived at my home and related his story to me, my heart was sad for him. He was suicidal and told me that he had every intention of killing himself. I became very nervous as I asked the Lord how to deal with this man. Jerry expressed that I was his final hope. I shuddered at his words and told him that I could not help him. I went on to explain that only Jesus had the power to change his life.

After much discussion, Jerry eventually became willing to ask Jesus to come into his life. As we prayed together tears flowed from his eyes. When he left he was noticeably more calm. I didn't know right then what would become of him, and felt somewhat relieved that he had gone.

Two days later Jerry appeared at my door with a broad smile on his face. As we chatted together over tea he told me that the day after he left my home he had received a letter from his daughter and an invitation to come and visit for Christmas. He had also secured a job with a firm that could use his talents and expertise. Jerry had called on Jesus, and the Lord had not been found wanting. My own faith was strengthened that day as we rejoiced in the love and mercy of God. The Holy Spirit is working!

Geraldine and I are continually aware of our ongoing spiritual formation. When we cooperate with the Holy Spirit we enter into God's direct will in a way that our temporal welfare is also affected for the better. One of the greatest lessons we have learned has been in the area of forgiveness. When I first experienced the love of Jesus in my life, I was finally able to forgive my father. Though I thought this was the end of my inability to forgive, the Lord could still see areas that had to be dealt with.

Some years ago a close friend had spread rumors and lies about me and had convinced my neighbors that I was evil. At the time we were holding a Catholic Sunday school in our home for children on the block. As a consequence of this man's verbal attack, the neighbors withdrew their children. For the next two years our family lived in isolation under a cloud of suspicion.

Often I wanted revenge. Desires to hurt this man who had slandered us dominated my thoughts. At the end of the second year, just before the annual community meeting, the Lord asked me to forgive him. I said it was impossible to forgive him from my heart. The Lord responded, "If you forgive him from your will, I will give forgiveness from the heart." I agreed.

The man who had spread the lies was leading the community meeting. When it was over I walked up and offered my hand in friendship. Before the whole community, he looked me in the eye and shouted, "Never!" I walked home angry and humiliated.

In a short while my neighbors, one by one, began to come to our home with cakes, biscuits, and apologies. They had all seen my clumsy gesture of friendship and this man's refusal to receive it. My neighbors felt that my effort at reconciliation did not live up to the description of me portrayed by my enemy.

True forgiveness began to pour from my heart as God had promised. Forgiveness first had to be a decision of my will before it could be transformed by God's love into forgiveness from the heart. God used this man to teach me the value of forgiveness. It wasn't long before he came to my door himself. I greeted him with joy. There was no need for him to ask forgiveness. Through God's grace, I had already forgiven him.

The fruit of forgiveness reaches far beyond our human understanding. I could not have known at the beginning of my trial that my willingness to forgive would touch the hearts of so many people. Neither could I have recognized those areas in myself that still needed healing until I was tested. When I decided to receive forgiveness for myself, I was set free. Had I chosen not to receive Jesus' forgiveness, I would have been held bound by the evil, captive to the power of the enemy.

Even further, holding onto unforgiveness, bitterness, resentment, and anger would have dishonored the shed blood of Jesus, made my life miserable, and possibly made my body sick. It would have been an act of incitement to my lost friend, causing him to sin through further acts of aggression. The only victor in our continuing estrangement would have been Satan, content with the destructive division that he had caused. I experienced that the fruit of forgiveness is freedom, joy, and peace, with a restored and stronger bond of unity.

I believe that when we go to confession after forgiving our neighbor we fulfill the requirements laid down in Scripture—to forgive our neighbor, to confess to one another, and to seek forgiveness from God for offenses committed against his love. I have never found a scriptural reference in the New Testament about private confession. The confessional itself is set in a public place. The priest through whom God administers absolution represents not only Christ himself but all the people of God. I am convinced that my healing was in a very real way associated with the confessional.

LOVE AND RECONCILIATION

Since the beginning of 1990 God has developed and further empowered my ministry. He has sent me out, fulfilling the promise he had made ten years before; to bring the good news to others. I now work full time in a ministry of love and reconciliation to God.

In October 1990 I was invited by Fr. Lannigan to speak at North Cathedral in Cork City. With many priests and the bishop of the diocese present, I was to speak on the Sacrament of Reconciliation. The tension was evident as I approached the podium. The celebrating priests were probably afraid that I would mess it up. As I approached the microphone I realized that this was a major turning point in my ministry. I looked down the aisles at all the people, then back at the tabernacle. The love of Jesus embraced me so tenderly that I had difficulty holding back the tears.

"I am with you," the Lord said. "Bring my people back." As I spoke I could see people crying at various locations throughout the church, and I knew the Holy Spirit was working. When the evening was over several priests were dispatched to handle the crowds that were lining up for confession. The priests could not believe the demand. Men and women who had been away thirty, forty, or more years were returning in tears.

As I watched in amazement, I remembered my own return and the growth that had taken form within me since that time. Here I was ten years later, a simple layman, speaking in the Cathedral in Cork City. I felt overwhelmed as the Lord said, "Brendan, you haven't seen anything yet."

Throughout years of hardship and pain, Geraldine has remained faithful to her marriage vows. Her selflessness and willingness to forgive created a climate where a change of attitude always remained open for me. I neither deserved nor expected such loving dedication. Yet in some strange way all during those terrible years, I had truly appreciated it.

In today's modern world, Geraldine is one of those unsung heroes who, despite all opinions to the contrary, refused to relinquish her responsibility. I believe that she would have been perfectly justified in doing so. God, however, who sees all, not only honored her dedication and commitment, but through conversion blessed it with a deeper sense of his love. Her love allowed us both to truly express the fullness of God's purposes within our marriage.

Geraldine is a strong love, disciplined and powerful, rising far above the mere outward gloss of fashionable sexual attraction and the momentary illusion of romantic infatuation. As a couple blessed in the union of marriage, we can honestly say that we deeply love each other. We will never be able to plumb the depths of that love in our lifetime. We pray that God will continue to bless us and extend his blessings to all families.

I pray that by reading this account you will be moved to turn to Jesus, regardless of your situation. Power, money, status, or sexual diversion can never bring security and dignity of purpose. Only Jesus can give those to you. He has a plan for your life that offers peace and the sure hope of salvation. In his plan for your life, you will discover your real self, your real purpose.

Jesus holds you in the palm of his hand and loves you without measure. He's just a call away. When I returned to him in my heart, Jesus responded with great love and compassion. He will do the same for you.

Highlights of Brendan's Story

- A friend invites Brendan to a prayer meeting.
- He receives the Sacrament of Reconciliation.
- He receives into his heart the Lord's word through the speaker at a prayer meeting.
- He receives prayer.
- He hears the Lord speak to him personally.
- He receives a vision of Jesus holding him and crying.
- He is baptized in the Holy Spirit.
- He experiences the love of Jesus.
- He receives the gift of tongues.
- He is healed in spirit, soul, and body.
- He asks forgiveness of his wife and children.
- He is obedient to the Holy Spirit who asks him to focus on his family's growth and conversion.

- He receives opportunities for growth in the area of forgiveness.
- He reaches out to give away what the Lord has given to him.

Prayer

Heavenly Father, I bring before you now those people who need to be reconciled with you. Perhaps like me, they came from homes of devastation and entered a life of self-destruction, never knowing the love and guidance of a mother and father. Perhaps they have escaped into drugs, alcohol, and sex to anesthetize themselves against the pain of life.

Father, heal the families. Give to the fathers an anointed gift of fathering, and give to the mothers an anointed gift of mothering. Turn the hearts of the fathers and mothers to their children, and the hearts of the children to their parents. Let healing and deliverance flow. Restore husbands and wives to their first love for each other. Let a gift of forgiveness flow between members of families. Strengthen your families, Lord. Bring new commitment and purpose to family life. Holy Spirit, reveal to them the meaning, the power, and the grace that flows from commitment.

Father, touch and heal your people. Place your healing hand on each person now as he or she prays this prayer. Pour your Holy Spirit into your people and give them a knowledge of how deeply they are loved. Let them know that in you there is hope, healing, and life without measure. Thank you, heavenly Father. Thank you, Jesus. Thank you, Holy Spirit.

Blessed Mother, please come and carry their cries to the throne of God. In Jesus' name I pray. Amen.

3

*Out of his infinite glory, may he give you
the power through his Spirit for your hidden self
to grow strong, so that Christ may live
in your hearts through faith, and then,
planted in love and built on love, you will
with all the saints have strength to grasp the
breadth and the length, the height and the depth;
until, knowing the love of Christ which is beyond
all knowledge, you are filled with the utter fullness
of God. Glory be to him whose power,
working in us, can do infinitely more than we can
ask or imagine; glory be to him from
generation to generation in the church and
in Christ Jesus for ever and ever. Amen.*

Ephesians 3:16-21 JB

THREE

That You Too
May Have Life

Sr. Eileen Jones

*Sr. Eileen Jones is a member of the Victorian Congregation of
the Sisters of the Presentation of the Blessed Virgin Mary. She
lives in Elsternwick, a suburb of Melbourne, Australia. Sr.
Eileen's experience of God's healing power reflects his great and
tender love. Her story will fill you with hope.*

GOD HAS WORKED POWERFULLY IN MY LIFE to bring healing and restoration. This Scripture passage from
Ephesians captures my prayer for all those who read of
his great and tender love as illustrated in the following
testimony.

My story begins in a special way in 1956. That September, I fell down a flight of stairs and damaged my
spine. Through a misunderstanding beyond my control, I waited three months for a bed in the hospital. At

the time I was teaching fourth and fifth grade. I will always be grateful for the loving response of those children as they witnessed my difficulty and frequent immobility.

The third eldest in a family of ten children, I have in many ways been involved in teaching all my life. I have especially tried to instill in my students over the years the deep faith I learned from my parents. That faith was to prove a lifeline in the many years of trials following my fall down the stairs.

The Mass and the sacraments were greatly appreciated in my family. Often during World War II when gas was rationed or unavailable, we rode ten miles in a horse-drawn vehicle to attend Mass in Boorhaman, instead of traveling by motor car to Rutherglen. Nothing would stop us from getting to Mass. My family gathered each night after the evening meal to pray the rosary together.

Often I witnessed the healing power of the Sacrament of the Anointing of the Sick, called the Sacrament of Extreme Unction in those days before Vatican II. My faith in the healing power of this sacrament was solidified when I watched my father, a soldier in World War I and an invalid in his later years, recover from various afflictions after being anointed by the priest.

Indeed, I thank God for the many times I have witnessed his healing power, both in my childhood and later after I joined the Presentation Sisters Novitiate in Elsternwick. This community was founded by Nano Nagle in Cork, Ireland, in 1775. Originally known as the Sisters of Charitable Instruction of the Sacred Heart of Jesus, this order taught me in secondary school, Mt. Carmel Convent in Rutherglen.

After my vows in 1950, I taught children in the primary grades for nearly twenty-four years. Many of those years were spent in small country schools, with four years as a principal in the country town of Chiltern. The remainder of my teaching career was spent in primary schools in the Melbourne suburbs. One of my great joys was serving as a sports coach, encouraging my students to get involved in outdoor sports and healthy activities. It was so easy for them to get into trouble if they had few outside interests. I love children very much and thank the Lord for allowing me to be an instrument of his healing love for them.

My students were especially loving toward me following my accident, when I was admitted to the hospital and put in traction. This was a very difficult period. While the nurses were kind, I felt there was something very wrong during the six days I spent in traction—set up by the specialist's nurse. I didn't know what to do about my fears. Finally, a different specialist examined me and ordered the traction removed. "It's not set up properly," he announced.

Two days later my spine was manipulated under an anesthetic. When that procedure failed, I was told there was nothing more that could be done. It was recommended that I wear a brace. During the next few years my spine was manipulated on several occasions.

ANOTHER ACCIDENT

Several years later in 1964, I was driving up Mount Hotham with my cousin at the wheel. Suddenly a car was coming down the hill on the wrong side of the road. While my cousin did everything he could to minimize the impact, I girded myself and thought, "We're going to be killed." We crashed head-on. I was still wearing my brace at the time, but my back sustained further injuries.

Two years later I lost the use of my right side and was sent to another specialist. Tests indicated that the nerves in my right leg and hip appeared to be dead, evidently because of pressure from my spinal injuries. After ordering X-rays he decided to try traction again. This time some flexibility returned.

Six months later he ordered physical therapy to strengthen the muscles in my back. The first exercise was so painful that the physical therapist reported it to the specialist, who then canceled the therapy and ordered further tests. These revealed that my spine had been injured in the traction in 1956. "There is nothing that can be done," he said. "You will be in a wheelchair in ten to fifteen years. All we can do is put you in traction every two years for the rest of your life, and give you medication for the pain."

This news was so devastating that I began to withdraw and isolate myself. I was the one who had encouraged the school children to get into sports and physical activities. Now I couldn't even sit for any length of time without pain unless I used a high, soft cushion.

No one, not even my superiors, seemed to understand what I was going through. In thinking through my trials years later, I came to realize that I had blocked the possibility of receiving help. My blockage began, I believe, with a judgment on my father. As a child I had concluded, "No matter what I do, I can never please him. No matter what my older sister does, she can never make a mistake in his eyes."

Later, our Lord was to reveal to me the importance of Matthew 7:1, "Do not judge, and you will not be judged; because the judgments you make are the judgments you will get." In the process of judging my father, I seemed to have put an unconscious judgment on all lawful authority, not allowing my superiors and others to believe or affirm me. I had become very resentful, feeling rejected and alone. I was convinced that people, especially those in authority, did not accept that there was anything seriously wrong with me.

In 1968, about two years after the doctor's verdict, I lost the use of my right side again. I decided, "If chiropractors can't do me any good, they can't do me any more harm." Over the following seven years my spine was manipulated many times, frequently twice a week. Since the steel brace was bent by this time, it was decided I would be better off without it. After 1967, I could no longer raise my arm above shoulder level to write on a chalkboard, so much of my teaching had to be confined to small groups or individuals. My hearing was tested in 1972. I learned that I had thirty-five percent hearing in one ear and only forty-five percent in the other. Even though I was going deaf, I never shared this fact with anyone. I had already judged that my friends and religious community did not accept I was an invalid and saw no point in saying any more. Deep inside, I was convinced that one day they would believe me, if only in eternity.

Because my eyesight was deteriorating, the prescription in my glasses changed every six weeks. I was also involved in another automobile accident. In 1973 I had major internal surgery as a result of the incorrect traction seventeen years earlier. The following year the chiropractors stopped treating me because my discs were too worn to hold.

I was sent to another back specialist. Feeling that I was only suffering from nerves after the previous year's major surgery, this doctor referred me to a psychiatrist. Even the twenty-seven daily tablets the psychiatrist prescribed failed to calm my nerves or deaden the pain. I continued in his care for two years, until he moved to another area.

As time went on, my mobility, hearing, and eyesight gradually diminished. In December 1976, after a nine hour eye examination that extended over two days, I was told, "Sister, you will be blind in less than two years. We can't save your sight." I cried out, "Lord, what do you want of me?" All I could really do was pray, even though I felt so little hope. Throughout this time I continued to believe that people would come to see that my suffering was not simply psychosomatic. Someday, my superiors would know the truth. By March 1977 I could not stretch my hands past my knees. I could see nothing clearly, even with my eyeglasses. The specialist told me at this stage, "Sister, it will only be a matter of weeks and you will not be able to see light or dark."

At this time I was receiving disability benefits and was instucted to apply for an invalid pension. However, our Lord knew the future and did not allow this to come through—despite the doctor's certificate. Perhaps it would have been difficult to convince the Social Security Department that I was no longer an invalid just two months later!

A MIRACULOUS RETREAT

During the May holidays I went to a directed retreat at the main house in our congregation. The priest giving the retreat said to me the first morning, "Eileen, we are going to pray about your back. When it is healed, it will be like a line of white fire burning through every nerve of your spinal system, bringing it back to life." At that time I had not heard of the charismatic gift of the word of knowledge.

During my interview time each day, the retreat director simply prayed for me. On the fourth day I looked up at him and said, "I can now forgive all my ex-superiors who did not believe there was anything wrong with me." I had finally acknowledged the judgment I had made on my father as a child, and how it had affected my relationship with authority figures throughout my life.

The retreat director replied, "Eileen, the Lord can now heal your spine." I could forgive, so now the Lord could heal. By his grace I had allowed the blockage to be removed.

The following afternoon during the first reading at the Eucharist, I felt my neck being jerked as though a chiropractor was putting it in place. I suddenly realized I could turn my head from side to side, for the first time in over two years. At the Prayer of the Faithful, the retreat director thanked our Lord for the most wonderful experience of his life. I learned later he was referring to the healing of my spine.

The next morning he said, "Eileen, the Lord is healing your spine in three sections. Remember, that was the way it was injured." As he prayed that day I saw a row of little white electric globes connected by fine wire, all lighting up one by one. By that afternoon I was sitting up straight in the chapel, in an ordinary chair and with no pain. When I realized my back was healed, I wept before our Lord. Forgiveness poured from my heart, along with a deep love for those people who had hurt me. I knelt down for the first time in eleven years.

That night I did not mind going without sleep, as one by one the nerves in my leg and hip came back to life. I could feel my leg growing to its right length so that I no longer needed my shoe to be built up inside. When the sun rose in the morning I could see everything in my room clearly, even without my eyeglasses. I heard my watch tick for the first time in seven years. Praise God!

When I told the priest he smiled, saying, "There is a lot more healing to come. If our Lord had totally healed you in an instant, you may have had a breakdown. You might not have been able to cope psychologically. Eileen, he has been very gentle."

I contacted the chiropractor who had attended me from 1971 to 1973 and asked if he would X-ray my spine again. Upon seeing the new X-rays, a month after the retreat, he said, "Sister, all the X-rays are yours as proof, if necessary." He added, "To those who do not believe, no explanation is possible. To those who believe, no explanation is necessary."

The eye specialist was astounded after preliminary tests confirmed my restored vision. He said, "Sister, I am an agnostic, but this is beyond any medical and scientific explanation. You should not be able to see at all!"

Prior to the retreat, I had made an appointment with the back specialist. When he asked how I was doing, I responded, "Tremendous!" He thought I had misunderstood him and asked again. Giving the same reply, I proceeded to stand up, bend over and touch the floor with my fingers, without bending my knees. I then offered to show him the X-rays taken in 1971, 1973, and 1977. After studying them for a long period he simply said, "Sister, I apologize for not X-raying your spine. I thought you were suffering from nerves as a result of your operation. But there was no way your spine could have healed—it was crushed. Come back and see me in three months."

When I returned three months later, he was amazed to see me so well. I simply said, "When our Lord heals, he does it properly." A few months later I saw this same back specialist again at his request. "Sister, you have traveled a long, hard road," he said that day. "But the Lord himself has healed you. If you ever need me again I will be happy to see you." I have not had any reason to go back.

I wish to emphasize the healing power of the Word

of God as it is proclaimed in the readings of the Mass. It was during the readings at the retreat that the first part of my healing took place. Then as I sat before our Lord in the Eucharist, I was conscious of my spine being healed. Our Lord gave me a great love for those who had not understood. I am also aware that healing takes place when the body gathers in praise and worship. Praise God, whose love can do so much more than we can ask or imagine.

GOD'S HEALING POWER

One day in 1984, a lady to whom I had been ministering expressed an urgent need to see me. On arrival she said, "I do not know why I am here, but felt I must come." We began to pray. At her request I started telling her the story of my healing. While doing so I accidentally mentioned the name of the back specialist who had injured my spine in the traction in 1956, bit my lip, and quickly continued.

The woman suddenly asked me to stop and repeat what I had said. When I repeated it without the name she said, "Sister, please tell me the name. It's important." As I spoke the name she burst into tears. "Sister, that man was my father." I knew he had died a year previously. The distraught woman said she was unworthy to hear the story sitting, and knelt on the floor. I did likewise. Both weeping, we asked forgiveness on behalf of the family—she for the damage done by the error and I for the bondage of resentment or unforgiveness that may still have been deep within.

That day I believe many people were set free. She told me that her father, a top orthopedic surgeon for many years, had been seriously overworked at the time and badly in need of a vacation. Her husband was also an orthopedic surgeon, also much in need of a rest. She would see that he took time off so that the mistake would not be repeated.

After my healing experience in 1977, I have been involved in the ministry of praying for healing for others, mostly inner healing. The more I pray for others, the more conscious I am of those areas in our lives that block the healing power of Jesus. In my estimation, these are some of the most significant areas of blockage: involvement in the occult, resentment and unforgiveness, judgments we have consciously or unconsciously made, our perceptions of how our parents acted toward us, generational sin, and hurts we received in the womb.

Once I went to visit my cousin in the hospital. An infection had formed following surgery for cancer, and Molly was in intensive care. About twelve months previously her son had died after being on a life-support machine. Their story had been used by the media and science as a case for discontinuing treatment to those on life support. The family had been persecuted over the ensuing months.

As we prayed, Molly was able to forgive those who had persecuted her. We then prayed for the healing of the infection, which left and never returned. About three months later, lumps appeared in her glands. The

Lord directed me to pray for the healing of trauma and shock. As we were praying together, the lumps disappeared under my fingers. On Molly's subsequent visits to the hospital there has been no further trace of cancer.

I believe that when we begin to pray for a healing, we need to go beyond praying for the effect and ask the Lord to show us the cause. Too often people have prayed for the healing of a headache without considering the cause of the pain.

Over a period of several years I have prayed with one particular family, conscious that much of the healing they needed was due to their involvement in the occult in past generations. People are often unaware that occult involvement has been a part of their family histories. Even if they become aware of this practice, they may not understand the dangers of opening the door of the spirit to the powers of darkness—perhaps under the guise of innocent fun, or simple games, or some other reason. Through prayer, this family has experienced the healing love of the Lord in many areas.

Once a young couple came to me for prayers for the woman's pregnancy, then in its seventh month. Their doctor was concerned that the baby had not grown in the previous month. When we prayed, I received a word of knowledge: "She told the baby to stop growing." The wife denied it. After prayer, I asked her, "When did you tell yourself that you must not get any bigger?" She said thoughtfully, "About a month ago when I realized I was getting uncomfortably large."

She then took back the statement, asked the baby to

forgive her, and gave the baby permission to grow. When she saw the doctor at eight months the baby was the expected size. A beautiful baby girl was born around the due date. Praise God! This showed us the receptivity of the baby's spirit. The environment in the womb is so sensitive.

One can't help but wonder; if a child feels rejected and unloved in later life, did the parents not want the child? This is not meant to condemn, but to face such a possibility in the presence of the Lord's forgiving love. Sometimes parents may simply question how they can cope with another child at a certain time. Those parents might want to ask God's forgiveness and, if appropriate, ask the child's forgiveness as well. Perhaps those who feel unwanted could forgive their parents and ask God's forgiveness for their own resentment.

Sometimes we may also experience resentment against God for being created at all. We can ask God's forgiveness for rebelling against life, in some cases even to the point of attempted suicide. If this is so, thank God for the gift of life and choose life (see Dt 30:19-21). Let's pray not only for the faith to believe our Lord has the power to heal us but also that he has the desire to heal us. Let's pray for an awareness of his incredible love.

One time I broke my wrist, shortly after I had heard a teaching on the whole area of believing and acting without doubting. I had been working all day on a recovery program at a shelter for homeless men, and had come home very late at night. Thinking about the heavy day ahead, I was walking up to my room when I heard the gate in the back yard banging in the wind. Knowing the noise would interfere with my sleep, I went downstairs again and into the yard.

The night was so dark that I didn't see a hole left by the plumber where he had been working. I fell into it and literally heard the bone snap in my wrist. Instantly, I was challenged to believe in the Lord's readiness to heal. Clasping my injured wrist with my other hand, I began praising and thanking God for the healing. I then went to bed and slept.

A few weeks later, when I was taking some senior sisters to a vacation house, I bent over and picked up some luggage. Suddenly, my wrist began to hurt. Later that day, some friends encouraged me to have it examined. The young doctor who came into the examining room with my X-rays seemed perplexed. "Sister, I can't get over this. You have had a very recent break in your wrist, a clean break, but I have never seen such a perfect knit."

The sister with me said, "She hasn't broken her wrist." I then explained what happened three weeks previously. The doctor replied, "Well, the Lord certainly healed the wrist perfectly." I knew then that God simply wanted me to have it verified so that I could continue to praise and thank him for his goodness. Let's ask God for expectant faith to believe his promises, and to believe that he loves us so much that he desires to heal us and free us from affliction.

God is a loving Father who desires to heal us more than we want to be healed. He is always ready to forgive, always ready to heal. Let's trust him to accomplish this in his perfect timing. There are many who have asked God for healing so many times, but are still waiting. Be patient with yourself, and with God.

As you pray the prayer at the end of this chapter, ask our Lord to show you the areas that need to be touched in your life, so that in his great love and mercy he may set you free to love and be loved more fully.

Highlights of Sr. Eileen's Story

- On retreat she receives a word of knowledge about her healing.
- The retreat director prays for her daily.
- She is able to forgive her former superiors.
- The Holy Spirit reveals to her a judgment she made against her father.
- Barriers to healing are removed when she forgives her father.
- She receives a further word of knowledge about the healing process.
- Evidences of physical healing begin to appear.
- There is X-ray documentation of healing of the spine.
- There is documentation of healing of her eyes.
- Healing occurs as she sits before the Lord in the Eucharist.
- Healing occurs as the Word of God is proclaimed at Mass.

- Healing occurs during praise and worship.
- With the daughter of the original surgeon, she is able to forgive him for the wrong he had done.
- She prays with others for healing.
- She communicates to others that God is a loving Father who desires to heal us more than we want to be healed.

Prayer

Lord, I come before you today and ask you to show me those areas in which I am most in need of your healing. Open my eyes to see the wounds in my life.

I forgive my ancestors for any lack of love or any inability to love, because they did not experience the love of their parents. Only you, Lord Jesus, can stand with your cross between me and my parents, and between my parents and grandparents, breaking the bonds of unlove, rejection, occult ties, or any other areas of darkness handed down through the generations. Thank you for setting me free.

I renounce all involvement in any practices associated with the occult, especially seances, ouija boards, fortune telling, tarot cards, horoscopes, charms, witchcraft, magic, and all other forms of the occult. I especially renounce _____.

Heavenly Father, I ask you to be present at my conception and heal me of any rejection, because there was not a true bond of love between my parents at that moment. No human love is perfect, so I ask you to bridge the gap between the love needed and the love received. Lord, fill me at the moment of conception with your perfect love.

Please release me from my judgment that I was not wanted, that I was a burden, that I was unloved. Forgive me and fill me with your love. I forgive my mother for not wanting to keep me. If, because of her rejection, I had a death wish in the womb, I take back that wish. Please forgive me, Father God. I choose life and thank you for the gift of life and the joy of living.

I take back my judgments against my father, perceiving that he didn't love me or that I could never satisfy him. I ask him to forgive me and I ask you, Father God, to forgive me and release my father from these judgments. I also take back any judgments I made against my mother and ask her to forgive me. I release her from these judgments today. (Even if your father or mother is dead, this is important.) Forgive me, Lord.

I ask forgiveness for the lie that I would always need to earn acceptance and repent of the perfection I have expected from myself and others. Lord, I ask that this lie be put to death on the cross and that I be released from its effects. I release all others I have entangled in this lie.

I ask you, Lord, to put to death on the cross the lie that I was a burden in my mother's womb. Release me from the lie that I would always be a burden, and always have to carry the burdens of others. Give me, instead, the gift of intercession, that I may intercede for those intentions you place upon my spirit, for the length of time you choose.

Lord, I forgive my brothers and sisters for the times they have hurt me. Give me your love for them. I forgive teachers, employers, priests, and religious who have hurt me or expected too much from me.

Lord, I ask you to walk gently through my life with me. Lord, show me the people I still need to forgive the most. Heal the wounds of the little inner child. Give me the courage to face the wounds, and allow your healing love to enter and heal me.

Come, Lord Jesus, and fill me with your love. Grant me the grace to love others. You have said, "Love yourself as I love you, and then love others as you love yourself." I ask for this grace to allow you to love me. Give me the grace, Lord, to accept your love and forgiveness. Enable me to love and accept myself and then be able to love and accept others.

Thank you, Lord, for your love. I accept your love. Thank you for loving and accepting me as I am. Amen.

4

... The Lord does not look at the things man looks at. Man looks at the outward appearance, but the Lord looks at the heart.

1 Samuel 16:7

Amazing Love

Fr. Joseph Whalen, M.S.

Fr. Joseph Whalen is a member of the Our Lady of La Salette missionary order, assigned to St. James Church in Danielson, Connecticut. The tender story of how the Lord lovingly drew this person from the pits of alcoholic degradation and into the holy priesthood is an inspiration for millions suffering from this disease, and those who pray for them.

M Y LIFE AS AN ALCOHOLIC began on the mud flats of Quincy, Massachusetts, when I was thirteen years old. In June 1976, I took my first sober breath in forty years. This is a miracle story, a love story, of how God took me out of the mud and the slime and brought me to the holy priesthood.

I told my spiritual director in the seminary, Fr. Paul Gilmartin, S.J., that I was the most unlikely candidate to become a priest. He responded, "Joe, don't talk like that. It's no mistake that you're here. God called you.

It doesn't matter what you think; it only matters what God thinks."

When I persisted, saying, "I'm just not good enough," Fr. Gilmartin responded, "None of us are good enough." I was reminded that God doesn't judge like ordinary human beings who see only the externals. God looks into the heart and sees our potential through the eyes of his eternal, unconditional, amazing love.

As I share my story with you, I pray that wherever you are or however bleak your circumstances may appear, you will realize that God will never, ever give up on you. He has a plan for your life. It has nothing to do with what you may think about your qualifications. It has everything to do with his amazing love.

I was born into a Catholic family on July 14, 1923, the oldest of seven boys. My mother wanted at least one of her sons to become a priest. When I was thirteen, my uncle, Bishop Georges Landry, spoke to me about going to Canada with him to study for the priesthood and promised to pay all my expenses. The thought of leaving my family made me very insecure, however, and I declined. I wanted no part of it. I wonder if the seeds of vocation were planted at that early age.

My father was a carpenter and out of work a lot during the depression years. I had been hustling a buck ever since I was ten years old, cutting hedges, mowing lawns, and selling newspapers in the summer to earn money for school clothes in the fall. In the winter I would shovel snow. My grandmother kept the earnings of all the boys in her silk stockings with runs in them.

To get a nickel out of her for a double feature movie was like pulling teeth.

My biggest money maker was digging clams, which I sold to a commercial dealer. Professional clam diggers gave me a flask of whiskey one time and challenged me to drink it straight. Before long I was spending the evenings sitting on the stone wall near Raccoon Island in Quincy Bay, drinking whiskey purchased by the town drunk.

One evening when I started walking the quarter mile home, the earth began to spin and I found myself in a cold sweat. The following morning I woke up with dry heaves in a vacant lot near the house. Sneaking quietly into the house I took off my shoes and headed up to the room shared with two of my brothers. Halfway up the stairs I heard my grandmother's voice. "Joseph, is that you? Where have you been? We had the police looking for you. We thought you had been kidnapped." Years later, when I was in recovery, I realized that I had suffered a blackout—a signpost to alcoholism.

In 1941, after graduating from Quincy High School, I joined the Navy and was sent to Portsmouth Naval Hospital for hospital corps training. My studies included anatomy, physiology, pharmacology, nursing, hygiene, sanitation, minor surgery, and first aid. I worked my way up from apprentice seaman to first-class pharmacist mate.

Eventually I received orders for overseas duty and was assigned to a submarine chaser. German subs were our target. My nickname aboard ship was "Doc," and I often accomplished tasks that doctors normally performed, because there were not enough medical doctors to go around.

One of my assignments as a pharmacist mate was to make cough medicine. When in port I would order a five gallon drum of 190 proof alcohol, supposedly for the cough medicine, then use most of it for instant gin. I took a glass beaker and glass rod and poured so many parts of 190 proof alcohol with distilled water and glycerine to make the liquid palatable and then added ten drops of juniper juice. Bang. Instant gin. Many nights I staggered back on board the ship with my clothes ripped or a shoe missing. Countless nights in nameless ports around the world I woke up in filthy, alcohol-stained clothes, too drunk to care where or how I slept.

After spending three years and three months in the U.S. Navy during World War II, I received an honorable discharge. Shortly after my return home to Massachusetts, I joined the U.S. Maritime Service. Following a period of training at Sheep's Head Bay in Long Island, New York, I obtained a maritime commission and became a purser with Moore McCormack Steamship Lines.

As an agent for the government we took relief supplies overseas, such as food to Trieste, Italy, or a load of coal up the River Seine to Le Havre, France. Besides running the medical unit, I assisted the captain in transporting advance money for the crew from port cities to the ship. This assignment required carrying a 45 revolver. During this period my drinking steadily increased. I had the shakes and I experienced more and more blackouts. I was a sick man.

DOWNWARD SPIRAL

After a year in the maritime service, I was hired by the New England Telephone company, a subsidiary of AT&T, as a central office equipment installer. By this time I was a married man with children. Over the next thirty-two years I worked my way up to a second level management position as an account executive in the sales and marketing department. It was a high stress, pressure cooker job.

I was going in two directions at once—upwards in my profession but in a downhill spiral spiritually, mentally, and physically. I was drinking myself to destruction. I was the source of such embarrassment that my five children were afraid to bring friends home. My wife, Frances, was always running interference and apologizing for my stinking behavior. I would slur my words and stagger around, yelling at everyone who crossed my path. My filthy mouth and obnoxious behavior sent everyone into hiding.

Someone once said that "God draws straight with crooked lines." I am overwhelmed by the way he has brought people into my life at just the right time to change the course of my life. Annie Freed, a mystic with a deep devotion to the Blessed Mother, played a significant role in my journey to the priesthood and specifically to the LaSalette Shrine. She introduced me to a cloistered nun, another mystic, Sr. Mary Michael of the Precious Blood Monastery in Manchester, New Hampshire.

At our first meeting, Sister looked deeply into my glazed, alcoholic eyes and said softly, "Joseph, I see you as a priest." Tears began to stream down my face. "What do you mean? You must be kidding!" I was bawling my eyes out as my mind fleetingly recalled my uncle's conversations with me in the summer of my thirteenth year. Amazing love.

Frances finally dragged me into court, where our marriage ended in a bitter divorce. In the heat of the court battle she said, "You'll end up in the gutter." All my life savings went up in smoke in the ensuing settlement. The anger and bitterness in my heart became as destructive as the alcohol.

I was loaded with guilt and remorse for my lifestyle and for my terrible behavior toward my wife and children. My soul was so stained, my actions so depraved, that I prayed to get cancer and die. I felt so rotten about myself that I just didn't want to live. I didn't see any way out except death. But God had something else in mind.

A friar at a Franciscan shrine near my office gave me the name of Fr. Lawler. I called for an appointment, not even knowing at the time that it was the Holy Spirit that was prompting me. I was simply desperate. When I walked out of my office that day, June 29, 1976, I almost turned the other direction and headed for the nearest bar. It was a powerful struggle, a moment of truth. But something propelled me to that life changing meeting.

A FELLOW ALCOHOLIC

Fr. Henry Vincent Lawler, an alcoholic and a Franciscan priest who had been sober eleven years at the time, was the most loving man I had ever met in my life. He radiated tremendous charisma, was soft-spoken, warm, and a good listener. I immediately took a strong liking to him. I was astounded and mystified when he told me that he, too, was an alcoholic.

Fr. Lawler's love and kindness broke down all my resistance. At one point when he put his arms around me I began to cry. His touch felt like a hug from heaven. Father said, "You're going to be okay, Joseph." I cried and cried as I told him how bad I felt because of all the things I had done to my wife and children. I asked, "How can I make it up to them?" He responded gently, "Right now, I'm not worried about your wife and family. I'm concerned about Joseph Whalen. We can consider them later."

This kindly priest spoke to me in a straightforward way about my alcoholism, focusing my attention on the disease rather than the moral issues with which I felt so overwhelmed. He told me that I had an illness and drew pictures of an escalator with arrows going up and arrows going down. He said I was on the down side of such an escalator—going down to destruction, killing myself with booze.

Fr. Lawler explained the path to destruction as three-fold, beginning with the spirit, followed by the mind, and then the physical body. This fellow alcoholic said that first a person would stop going to church. Two drinks and nothing mattered. All inhibitions would be gone. Then the mental deterioration would come. A person could expect to become preoccupied with catastrophes, filled with guilt, and even afraid to answer the phone.

All this was familiar to me. I was also on the verge of D.T.'s (*delirium tremens*). I would shake and see strange things like bugs crawling out of the walls. He told me that the third stage would be bleeding ulcers or cirrhosis of the liver, and possibly even death.

He said that the arrow up, the path to recovery, would have to come in the reverse order. The first step would be physical. When people stopped abusing alcohol, they would begin to feel better physically, which would then affect their mental outlook. When the recovering alcholic was gaining physical strength and mental clarity, the spiritual dimension would begin to improve.

This distinction between body, mind, and spirit is not very clear cut. God certainly works uniquely in each of our lives and I deeply respect the variety of his ways. But the process I describe is what Fr. Lawler shared with me and what has proven true in my own recovery. He further told me that once he made a decision to stop drinking, it took him five years to get his head screwed on straight. He reminded me kindly that the path would be rough, and there would be setbacks. But there would be people to help.

One of the most important things I learned from this gentle, loving man was faith and belief in prayer. I had no faith. I was convinced any prayer I attempted would evaporate into thin air and never get beyond the telephone wires. Somehow the reality of Fr. Lawler's faith and relationship with God were communicated to me.

I also learned about forgiveness from him. He told me to "keep it simple" and to "maintain an attitude of gratitude." With my morning and evening prayers, he told me to say three simple words whenever bitterness and resentment would creep in: "God bless Frances"— or whoever happened to be the object of my displeasure. This simple prayer helped me through many painful months of unforgiveness toward myself, my wife, my boss, the world. It helped me get up and start over when I stumbled and fell.

Fr. Lawler took me to my first Alcoholics Anonymous (A.A.) meeting in the basement of St. Elizabeth's Church in Milton, Massachusetts. By the end of the evening he said, "Joseph, I was talking to the others. They all agree with me that you are going to make it. They say it's because you have such an open mind. You accept my suggestions. You are going to make it."

In the weeks and months to come Fr. Lawler would call me regularly at work and ask me how I was doing. He would say in his soft, loving voice, "Did you drink today, Joseph?" He always called me Joseph. When I said, "No," he would respond, "Then you will have a good day." Once this wonderfully loving priest said, "Just think, Joseph, how the Lord Jesus is looking down from heaven and smiling as you put your head on the pillow at night. I can just hear him saying, 'Well done, my good and faithful servant. You didn't drink today.'"

On the day of my first meeting with Fr. Lawler, June 29, 1976—the feast of Sts. Peter and Paul—I had my last drink. Many people over the years had told me I had to quit drinking. It had to come from the right person, however. Fr. Lawler also heard my first confession in fifteen years. He told me to go to church and talk to Jesus at the altar. And I did. I fell on my knees and surrendered to him, as best I could. That's when I started back to church.

Fr. Lawler told me it was important to get on my knees first thing in the morning and ask Jesus to help me stay away from alcohol that day. He advised me to end the day in the same way, with a prayer of gratitude for an alcohol-free day. He promised that the Lord would help me, one day at a time, as I placed my trust in him.

THE LONG ROAD TO RECOVERY

Just as it took Fr. Lawler five years, it also took me five years to recover from alcoholism. Often I would take two steps forward and three steps back before I was solidly on the path to victory. There were times I almost crawled out of my skin, I was shaking so badly with withdrawal. Other times I would read a sentence over and over and couldn't remember what I read. I would say things backward. I would get tongue-tied. My brain was like scrambled eggs because of the alcohol. When my mind eventually began to clear, I began to grow spiritually.

In 1978 Chuck Costa, a former Boston policeman who later became my A.A. sponsor, invited me to a charismatic prayer meeting at St. Ambrose Parish in Dorchester. He had to ask me several more times before I finally agreed to go. The first thing I announced when we arrived at the meeting was that I didn't believe in all that jumping around and "praise you, Jesus," stuff. I told him I was only there because I promised him I would go, as I was a man of my word. Chuck just smiled.

A member of the prayer group, Alice Matchem, who works for Cardinal Bernard Law at the Conference of Bishops in Boston, encouraged me to stay with the prayer group. She understood my drinking problem and often saw me at my worst, but kept encouraging me whenever I was ready to drop out. It was through Alice that I began to associate with religious people, whereas before I spent my time with alcoholics. She would invite me to her home for dinner and take me to religious functions. A holy and loving lay person, Alice broadened my horizons and helped me to experience the loving nature of God.

When I was eventually baptized in the Holy Spirit, it was not a dramatic experience, yet something started to change at a deep, foundational level. The Spirit of God was at work, drawing me, wooing me, capturing my heart. Amazing love.

Dr. Frank Downey was another powerful influence in my journey toward the priesthood. An alcoholic who studied seven years to become a priest of the LaSalette missionary order, he eventually left to marry and became a doctor. Often during A.A. meetings he would throw out pearls of wisdom. When I asked him the source, Frank said the truths came from the Bible.

Encouraged by him, I went out and bought a New American Bible and began reading it from cover to cover. The Holy Spirit began to fire up in me an intense desire for wisdom and knowledge. This fire was burning inside like it burned in the two men on the road to Emmaus in Luke 24. Then I began reading books about angels, the Lives of the Saints, and Summa Theologica, Volume 2. I even took over four hundred pages of notes from treatises by St. Thomas Aquinas. One that I remember quite well was the treatise on natural law, which St. Thomas defines as "do good, pursue it, and avoid evil." I didn't know until later how all this would help me later in philosophy courses in the seminary.

In 1983, I began getting visions. After prayers, with my eyes closed but before going to sleep, I would first see pinpoints of light, then whole fields of brilliant bluish light, pulsating like a kaleidoscope. Then the visions would disappear. I would say, "God, what was that?" The visions continued every night for seven months after prayer.

Sometimes I would see Jesus suspended from the cross, one heart with two thorns around it, or two hearts with thorns around them. Many times I would see a big white dove heading toward me as the field of vision became an intense blue-white. On frequent occasions I would see a dazzling white cross with no corpus. In the last vision I saw two angels suspended with their wings fluttering and a dove gliding toward them. All these visions were in brilliant color with great sweeping movements.

As I was checking all this out with a Franciscan priest, a former novice master for the Franciscan friars in Silver Spring, Maryland, I remembered a friend's prayer. Charlene Schafer, S.P.S., was a Sister of the Holy Spirit in Technay, Illinois, who often wrote to give me encouragement. She once told me she had prayed for me to receive visions. This wise old priest told me that I was receiving consolation to draw me into the religious life.

All this occurred when I was living in an apartment in Dorchester, Massachusetts, and going through a regression—a sinful and shameful period in my recovery. I had retired from my position in the phone company in December 1982, and was floundering around, not knowing what to do with my life. The Holy Spirit would draw me to the Lord, then I would pull away and head back into darkness. I felt like I was standing on the edge of an abyss with all my bridges burned.

GOD TALKS TO AN ALCOHOLIC

One night in the apartment in Dorchester, I woke up at three o'clock in the morning and felt like I was inside the core of the sun. When I came to my senses I realized that the house was on fire. In that peak experience when I was almost burned to death and my life was hanging on a thread, I finally responded to the call from God. It was like an inner voice. I simply knew God was calling, and I said yes.

I can look back now and see it was the Holy Spirit putting in my mind the words, "1 Corinthians 1:26-31." I couldn't get it out of my head. I tossed and turned all night, wondering what this was all about. It never occurred to me that God was speaking to me through that reference. A few days later when I was getting ready for bed, I picked up my New American Bible and read this passage. Tears began rolling from my eyes.

> Brothers, you are among those called. Consider your situation. Not many of you are wise, as men account wisdom; not many are influential; and surely not many are well born. God chose those whom the world considers absurd to shame the wise; he singled out the weak of this world to shame the strong. He chose the world's lowborn and despised, those who count for nothing, to reduce to nothing those who were something; so that mankind can do no boasting before God. God it is who has given you life in Christ Jesus. He has made him our wisdom and also our justice, our sanctification, and our redemption. This is just as you find it written, "Let him who would boast, boast in the Lord." (NAB)

It was as if the Holy Spirit was speaking these words directly into my life. When I finished reading it I was bawling like a baby. I said, "Almighty God, Jesus, I will never doubt you again. I know you are calling me to the priesthood." The all powerful God was talking to me, Joe Whalen, a little punk, a boozer. He was talking to me personally, calling *me* to his holy priesthood. Mine had been the most unholy life of any person I had ever known.

It was a miracle that God would even talk to me, much less tell me I had such a calling. I was so stupid at first that I didn't even realize he was talking to me! Gradually, day by day, I was beginning to realize that God was in charge. I didn't have to get my life sorted out on my own. Something greater was at work on my behalf. Amazing love.

On the same day of the fire I received in the mail an enrollment in the Association of the Holy Spirit from the Sisters of the Holy Spirit Convent in Technay, Illinois. This seemed like a further confirmation of God's calling.

My thirty-four-year marriage was officially annulled through the Boston Tribunal Office, based primarily on my alcoholism. Inspired by Dr. Frank Downey, I applied for admission in the Missionaries of Our Lady of LaSalette, a society with a charism of reconciliation. Annie Freed confirmed this direction one day, saying, "Joe, this is where you belong." To my great joy, I was accepted. My acceptance set a precedent because I was older than the normal cut-off age. The provincial convinced the vocation council that my priesthood was an action of the Holy Spirit and that I would not be a liability to the order.

People who didn't see the action of the Holy Spirit

quite so clearly said the idea of my becoming a priest was crazy. The obstacles seemed insurmountable. But one by one the Lord removed the obstacles, including an impossible $15,000 debt. He even took away my cigarettes. I had smoked two packs a day of unfiltered Camels from age thirteen. At an A.A. meeting early in 1980 I had my last cigarette.

My prayers for God to "melt me, mold me" were being answered. I was in the hands of the Master Potter. In 1982 my income was forty thousand a year. In 1983 my income dropped to one hundred dollars a month. Yet it was the most sensible move of my life!

Following six months as a postulant and a year in the novitiate in Washington, D.C., I spent another year at the University of Massachusetts and four years in graduate studies at Pope John XXIII National Seminary in Weston, Massachusetts. At the seminary I was the only one in the class of nineteen that was a divorced alcoholic with only a high school education!

I felt really out of place, a dummy with all those men with master's degrees. Some were former teachers and professors, one was a medical doctor, another was the vice president of a large department store. I always felt inferior. All my life I had struggled with low self-esteem and lack of self-confidence. Yet the grace of God was with me and I did well in my studies. Fr. Paul Gilmartin finally convinced me that no one is good enough. It's all God's grace.

Cardinal Bernard Law ordained me a deacon on January 28, 1989. On September 9, 1989, at the tender age of sixty-six, I was ordained a Roman Catholic priest by Boston's Auxiliary Bishop, Alfred Hughes. Amazing love.

THE GIFT OF RECONCILIATION

Reflecting back, my mother died twenty-five years before I was ordained a priest. I am convinced that her prayers had much to do with my fulfilled vocation. When I visited Sr. Mary Michael again she said, "Joseph, I am convinced that your mother got a glimpse of your ordination. Jesus surely parted the skies to allow her to look down from heaven and see the fulfillment of her prayers."

My former wife had also prayed for me and is at peace with me today. I have been freed from the resentment toward her and also pray for her. The grace of God has washed away the bitterness and the anger between us, to the point where a gentle, comfortable friendship has emerged. She said in a note after my ordination, "Joe, I am so proud of you, and so happy for you."

My pension from the telephone company is held in trust to provide for her needs and the needs of the children. I do not receive a penny. It is a good arrangement. My relationship with my oldest son, Mark, is friendly. We have stayed in touch over the years. Perhaps, in time, my other four children will be able to forgive me for all the pain I have caused in their lives and be open to a relationship with me. I pray for them daily.

In July 1989, I was assigned to the National Shrine of Our Lady of LaSalette in Ipswich, Massachusetts. During my time there I was spiritual director of the prayer group that meets at the Shrine and would occasionally fill in for Fr. Edward McDonough in Watertown when he traveled on trips connected to his healing ministry. In fact, I was able to fill in for him in a memorable trip to Medjugorje, Yugoslavia, and said Mass in St. James Church with about five thousand people present. Fr. McDonough also recommended me for a healing Mass at St. Anthony's Shrine in Boston. I am overwhelmed by the doors that are opening.

What I like best is ministry to alcoholics, which I am continuing on my new assignment at St. James Church in Danielson, Connecticut. I especially appreciate the twelve steps of A.A. as valuable tools in recovery. A great deal of my time with alcoholics is spent working with them on their fifth step, which is admitting to God and another person the nature of their wrongdoing. I catch a lot of big fish with this one, often restoring to the Sacrament of Reconciliation Catholics who have been away for twenty to thirty years. I have a ninety-nine percent success rate in converting this step into confession.

There is a saying that when a guy gives up something to help another person he divides his problems and multiplies his success. Paul Russell gave me the opportunity to repay what I had received from God. Paul asked me to be his A.A. sponsor and later gave me the privilege of giving him his first communion when he was converted to Catholicism. Today Paul is my closest friend.

Isn't it miraculous what God has accomplished in my life? When everybody had written me off as an incurable drunk, our Lord Jesus Christ saw my potential. Through his loving mercy, kindness, compassion, and power, God raised me to his holy priesthood and gave me gifts of healing for other broken lives. There are not enough words in the English language to describe our Lord's amazing love.

Highlights of Fr. Joe's Story

- Sr. Mary Michael prophesies that Joe will become a priest.
- The Holy Spirit prompts him to call Fr. Lawler.
- Fr. Lawler's love and affirmation break down his resistance.
- Fr. Lawler communicates to him a faith and belief in prayer.
- He learns forgiveness through Fr. Lawler.
- He learns about the importance of gratitude through Fr. Lawler.
- He is led to join Alcoholics Anonymous.
- He receives the Sacrament of Reconciliation.
- He goes to a charismatic prayer meeting.

- He learns more about the loving nature of God.
- He is baptized in the Holy Spirit.
- He developes a thirst for Scripture.
- He becomes aware of a drawing toward the priesthood.
- In a moment of crisis, he responds to a call from God.
- The Holy Spirit speaks words of healing and promise directly to his life.
- His vocation is confirmed.
- The Lord removes all obstacles.
- Peace is established with his former wife.
- He begins reaching out to other alcoholics.

Prayer

Merciful God, you are a loving, kind, generous, powerful God, slow to anger and rich in compassion. All merciful Jesus Christ, I pray that you will use me, one day at a time, to be a witness of your amazing love to the whole world. You brought me up from the pits of despair, from the filth of the gutter, into your holy priesthood.

Lord Jesus, no job is too tough for you. Everyone gave up on me when I was a drunk, yet you didn't judge me like ordinary human beings who see the external and say, "Get away from that filthy drunk. He's no good." You never said that, Jesus. Your divine ways are not like man's ways. You see a person's potential. In my case you saw my potential—not a filthy mouthed, obnoxious drunk.

Lord Jesus, I can look back now at the events in my life and see clearly, step-by-step, how you lovingly and patiently brought the right people into my life at the right time. You always had everything under control.

Lord, I am fully aware that this is just the beginning. I have so much to learn from you. I feel deep within my heart that you want me to witness to your amazing love to the whole world. Allow me, through your grace and the intercession of Our Lady of LaSalette, your mother, to be that witness, especially to those suffering from alcoholism. Let me always place the needs of the sick and suffering alcoholic before my own comfort.

Help others to see that if I can be ordained at sixty-six, with my background of depravity, addiction, and self-destruction, then anything is possible with you. It was clearly the power of your grace that gave the enlightenment and energy to accomplish this transformation.

Lord Jesus, I am so grateful for what you have done. Gratitude is a mountain of virtue. Without gratitude I cannot love you, myself, or my brothers and sisters. I know that nothing is coincidence, and that you sent me to the Shrine as a part of your plan. Let me never fail in my gratitude to you for your work in and through me.

St. Paul tells us that the greatest gift is love (1 Cor 13). That is what you have given me—abundant love. The bottled-up love in my heart is overflowing. The desire to express that love is burning brightly. Tell me what to do, Lord Jesus, and I will do it.

Lord, I pray now for the people who have helped me along the way. I am filled with gratitude for each of them, those I have mentioned and the many others too numerous to name. Lord, return a hundredfold blessing to each of them for the gift they have been to me.

Lord, I pray for those who you are calling to reach out to suffering alcoholics and others in need. Strengthen them, Lord. Give them courage to respond. Ignite in them a deep love and compassion for the downtrodden, the broken, the lost.

Lord Jesus, I pray now for the people I have hurt along the way because of my alcoholism. Please continue to heal the wounds I have caused to my former wife and my children. Let them not turn away from you because I was a bad role model. Please make up the difference between the love they needed and the poor love they received from me. Give them the grace of forgiveness, healing, love, peace, and joy. Thank you, Lord, for removing any remaining hostility and pouring in your healing love.

I pray now for those reading this book who are trapped in addiction, especially to alcohol. Whether you are a skid row bum or a corporate executive, a housewife or a hooker, stop and listen. Jesus loves you and has a plan for your life. People are praying for you. I am praying for you. Do not throw your life away. You may feel that it is too late to do anything worthwhile. You may feel that your life has become so degraded that it can never become healthy and productive again. When you start to feel that way, please reread my story.

What God has done for me, he will do for you. You are precious and valuable, a priceless treasure.

You may be saying, "I just can't make it. The spirit of booze is too strong." I say to you now that the Spirit of the living God is stronger than any alcoholic spirits. Lord, let your Spirit come like a mighty wind, right now, into those who feel hopelessness and despair.

You may be saying, "I can't do it alone." I know that. Jesus knows that. You are not alone. Stop right now and ask Jesus for help. Surrender to him as Lord of your life. He will guide you to the help you need.

I pray that the life-changing power of the Holy Spirit will come upon you now, at this very moment. Lord, do whatever is needed to bring wholeness to each person who has heard my story. Thank you, Lord, for your amazing love. Amen.

5

---

*"I will be a Father to you, and you
will be my sons and daughters, says
the Lord Almighty."*

2 Corinthians 6:18

5

Miracles of the Heart

Linda Schubert

Linda Schubert is active in the charismatic renewal in the Diocese of San Jose, California, and is especially involved in writing, teaching, and prayer ministry. In the following testimony, she shares the deeply intimate experience of how her relationship with her father was healed. Linda's many personal tragedies and triumphs on her path to the Lord were described to her as "golden." God says in Jeremiah 31:3: "... I have loved you with an everlasting love;..." He is also leading you on a golden path, and your future is filled with love.

ONE LABOR DAY WEEKEND I arrived at the Anaheim Convention Center in Southern California for a regional charismatic convention, wondering why I was there. My father, two hours away at my sister's home in Escondido, was dying.

I didn't hear a word spoken by Fr. Robert DeGrandis or any of the other convention speakers. All during the weekend my attention was glued to a young couple with their small daughter. The child looked deeply into her father's eyes and snuggled up against his chest in total contentment. He in turn drew his daughter close and looked at her with so much love it was breathtaking.

Later, at the closing Mass, it finally dawned on me; that was the way I related to my father when I was her age. The realization made me dizzy. I don't know when my relationship with Dad had changed. The moment I closed myself off to him is buried deep in my unconscious. But at some point I erected a barrier between myself and my father, and when I did so it seemed to affect my relationship with all men.

As far back as I can remember, I have been afraid to look deeply into a man's eyes, unable to open my spirit to a man, or feel comfortable and free in a man's presence. Every male relationship has been difficult, contaminated by feelings of distrust. Even a casual touch would often trigger fear. Fear and insecurity have dominated my life as long as I can remember. In some ways I have been like a tight little rosebud struggling to protect myself, unable to open and freely bloom. God's fatherly role in leading me from rosebud to rosebloom, from fear to faith, is central to this story.

When I was a child our family owned a 2400-acre ranch with a redwood lumber mill, high above the fog in the Santa Lucia mountains along the coast of northern California. The Bear Trap Lumber Company—designed, built, and operated by my father—provided Monterey County with quality lumber for the construction business. Dad's logging trucks made regular trips down the five miles of steep, narrow gravel road to the highway, then up the coast past Palo Colorado School and into town. In the 1940s the little white schoolhouse on Highway One had sixteen children in six grades, all in one room. That is where I received my early childhood education.

Dad was a rough outdoorsman, a stubborn, stoic Dutchman, a silent father. He had an eighth-grade education, was almost totally deaf, blind in one eye, and walked with a limp from a logging accident that had crushed his leg. My father had been rejected as a soldier in World War II because, among other things, he was missing his "trigger finger." He seemed to be a magnet for traumatic experiences. Dad also proved to be an unsuccessful businessman. Time after time he went bankrupt, leaving mother to pick up the pieces and return to teaching school to support the family until he tried some new venture.

Dad and I were alike in many ways. I, too, am stubborn, introverted, and prone to traumatic experiences. I, too, am creative, artistic, and insistent upon quality craftsmanship. I, too, prefer the freedom that self-employment offers, yet possess limited business skills. I, too, have been through bankruptcy and tend to focus more on the craft than the money. Those are but a few of our similarities.

I had no Christian upbringing. Dad was an atheist and the son of an atheist, while his mother was deeply involved in the occult. Mom came from a long line of Episcopal priests on her father's side, her father himself a Christian man who loved Jesus. But her father's death when she was a child shut her off from Christian influences. She had a personal encounter with Christ in college, but kept her faith a secret because of her mother's antagonism toward religious experience.

As I look back, I know that God was always with me. My mother says that I "came in on prayer" because my safe birth was such a miracle. After being carried in the womb for ten months, I was delivered by caesarian section at thirteen pounds! Dr. Hathaway said I was in every way a month old when I was born. The hand of God seemed so strongly upon us during the pregnancy that Mom had the sensation of being enclosed in heavenly white light and filled with a deep peace.

My clearest knowledge of Jesus came through a song someone taught me when I was quite young. On a grassy slope sprinkled with wildflowers and California poppies, a rope swing hung from an ancient oak tree beside our rickety old farmhouse. I would climb onto the swing in my faded bib overalls and scuffed brown shoes and pump very hard, swinging high up into the branches of the oak tree.

With the wind and the sun in my hair, I would tilt my head back and sing, "Jesus loves me, this I know, for the Bible tells me so. Little ones to him belong, they are weak, but he is strong. Yes, Jesus loves me. Yes, Jesus loves me. Yes, Jesus loves me. The Bible tells me so." In retrospect I realize those hours on the swing were the most peaceful and beautiful moments of my childhood.

When I was in the sixth grade, our ranch was sold after a fire set by an arsonist burned the forest and the mill, as well as killed two people. Uninsured and nearly broke, we moved to Pacific Grove, then to Oroville, then to the Palm Springs area—wherever Dad could find contracts in construction. By the time I graduated from high school, I had lived in a dozen places. I was an awkward country girl with no social skills, thrown into city schools and city ways, with no place that really felt like home. Relating to people was difficult and every failure built another layer of ice around my heart.

DEATH AND SEX

When I was a junior at San Jose State College I married a man named Bill. Physically abandoned by his father as an infant and emotionally abandoned by an alcoholic mother, he was raised primarily by his grandfather. In some ways we were like two rootless children looking for a place to belong.

After our wedding, Bill became increasingly preoccupied with locating the father he had never known, spending hours on the phone following up leads. He finally thought he had found him. I'll never forget the sound of his voice when he said to a man in Atlanta, Georgia, "This is your son, Bill." I sold my grandmother's piano to afford the train fare for him to go to Georgia, then dropped out of school a few weeks later and followed him. We struggled for six months to develop a relationship with this man, then decided to come home, saddened by a deep sense of failure.

We were on our way back to California, traveling by

train through Texas on Easter Sunday in 1959. I was in a strange state of mind—still grieving, sorting out the pain and the loss of what might have been. I'm embarrassed to tell what happened next, but it has a bearing on my reaction to a tragedy that was about to unfold.

After having a drink in the club car, Bill and I went into a restroom and had sexual relations. I could hear the train whistle as we passed over a long, high bridge. It was a beautiful sunny day and families were gathered for an Easter picnic by the river. Suddenly the train screeched to a halt. The shocking scene outside the window irrevocably changed the course of my life.

Six children had been walking along the railroad trestle, while their families visited beside the river below. The train came upon them without warning. One young boy jumped to the ground far below and broke a leg but survived. The remaining five children were killed. Fragments of their bodies were strewn all over the dry Texas grass beside the train. The terrible trauma of that bloody scene penetrated to the depths of my being and sorely wounded my spirit. I would never be the same person again.

Within a few weeks of our arrival in California, I ran away and left Bill. After obtaining a Reno divorce, I immediately jumped into a marriage with a boyfriend from high school. A year later I ran away and left him too. I made a vow never to have children. Sex and death had become irrevocably intertwined in my mind. I seemed to have had an emotional breakdown, but didn't receive professional help until years later.

I became very hard and developed a cutting edge to

my personality. With a sharp glance, I could slice a person in two. People were afraid of my harsh, angry tongue, and gave me a nickname of "Deadly." I shut everyone out of my inner life, including my family, and walked alone in the midst of a crowd of people.

At twenty-five I married a man with four children and began raising them three years later, when they were ages six, eight, ten, and twelve. I never did have a child and never let my step-children really know me. I cut off every offer of assistance from my family and was often more affectionate with our Siamese cat than with the children.

The year the children came to live with us, my husband expressed the desire for our family to become Catholic. We all submitted to his decision and began a course of preparation. The pastor of our parish, Our Lady of the Rosary in Palo Alto, told us that because of our marital history we would have to join the church as brother and sister. We did so in 1965, and lived together celibately for the remaining twenty-two years of our married life.

My stepson, Randy, contracted a rare, incurable form of muscle and tissue cancer at age seventeen. After a three-year respite, he began a battle for his life. Randy died on August 12, 1977, at age twenty-one. One morning about a week before he died, I was in his room preparing a morphine injection. He suddenly looked up at me and asked, "Mom, how do you feel about me?" My love was trapped inside and only the empty words came out: "You know I love you."

Truthfully, Randy was his father's boy and I had to

keep my hands off. I didn't know how to express my love anyway. Only later after his death—when I was finally learning how to love—could I pour out my true feelings to him. But that wasn't when Randy had needed it the most.

A NEW BEGINNING

At about this same time my mother went to a Women's Aglow meeting and received a prophetic sense from the Lord. Mom wrote to me in a letter: "The prophecy stated that the child I'd been worried about for so long was okay, and that I would hear in about three months. The prophecy pierced me. I knew that you were okay. [The prophet's] word fit with a vision I'd been having about you for nearly a year. I saw you on a winding golden path. The image was clear, and I saw it often. You were on the path he had chosen, and it was golden."

The turning point in my life came a few days after Randy died. One afternoon, I was as low emotionally as I could possibly get. I switched on the television to a program I had never watched before. Pat Robertson on the 700 Club was beginning a prayer. I fell crying to my knees and joined him in praying something like this:

Lord Jesus, I confess to you that I am a sinner. I believe you died for my sins. I ask your forgiveness for all the ways I have not honored you and turn away from my sins. I open my heart to you and ask you to come in and be Lord of my life. I receive you as my Lord and Savior. Please fill me with your Holy Spirit. Thank You, Lord. Amen.

Little did I know the difference that simple prayer would make. All my life I had been struggling in my own energy to get my life to work and I had always failed. From earliest childhood I had been taught the importance of self-sufficiency. That life-changing afternoon, a couple of months before my fortieth birthday, I learned about God-sufficiency.

That prayer brought deep changes. For one thing, I felt a profound sense of belonging, whereas before I had always felt like I was on the outside looking in. I didn't feel alone anymore. I felt accepted and loved and satisfied at the very core of my being. And I discovered, finally, that I wasn't even supposed to try and get my life to work in my own energy. God had a better plan. The Holy Spirit was given to show me the way and provide the energy to get there.

The Lord released the gift of tongues the same day with no instruction, no laying on of hands, without my even asking. This new way of praying just came bubbling out. It was an awesome, unforgettable day. Entering into a personal relationship with Jesus and experiencing baptism in the Holy Spirit was the beginning of my healing. I began to love the church as I had never believed possible and felt very grateful that my husband had insisted upon our joining.

Something inside could no longer handle the isolation that was so familiar to me. So I began asking the

Lord for friends. Some warm, safe, enduring friendships with women began to unfold. Through them I began to learn the meaning of Christian community. I wondered how I had made it so long without a Christian support group.

When Randy died, I was overflowing with the consolation of God's love but my family seemed to be falling apart. My second stepson became schizophrenic and my husband had a nervous breakdown and was on disability for a year. I stood with my head and heart in heaven—on the one hand filled with joy, but on the other hand shocked and traumatized by the devastation in my family.

God's graces were poured into me. He had promised, "I will not leave you as orphans; I will come to you" (Jn 14:18). I discovered that I could expect him to help me work through the complex, painful emotions surrounding the death of Randy. I could ask for help when I would get flashbacks about standing on the mountain at midnight when I was twelve, watching the wall of fire race through the hills. I didn't have to stay locked into the train trauma, either, because he had promised never to leave me desolate.

I read in Scripture that "... we are more than conquerors through him who loved us" (Rom 8:37). I began to reach out to the Holy Spirit to conquer anxiety when my husband couldn't even handle the stress of answering the telephone following his breakdown. And when the police carried away my schizophrenic stepson to a psychiatric facility in a straitjacket, the Holy Spirit taught me what it meant to be a conqueror.

The Lord makes a tremendous promise: "For I know the plans I have for you [the golden path]... plans to prosper you and not to harm you, plans to give you hope and a future" (Jer 29:11). I realized that I didn't have to stay trapped in dark memories, such as my experience as an eight-year-old girl sexually abused in the barn by an eighteen-year-old family friend. One time not too long ago the Lord gave me a vision of myself as a young girl hiding under a kitchen table. The Lord appeared beside the table and reached out his hand to draw me out. I was wearing a dirty white dress. As I crawled out, I heard the words "Little girl dressed in shame." Then as I stood beside the Lord I was wearing a yellow-dotted swiss party dress. In his presence I began twirling around the room, filled with life. The shame was gone.

I realized that the evil I had experienced in my life did not come from God. No, he is the author of restoration and hope. Someone once described the Christian life as God's "refinishing school." God reminded me that I am carved on the palm of his hand. He was restoring and rebuilding my life. He had wonderful things in store for me.

In the period following my deep encounter with the Lord and the experience of being baptized in the Holy Spirit, I began soaking up every teaching, workshop, seminar, and book on healing that I could find. I spent hours in prayer, hours reading Scripture. I listened to dozens of teaching tapes and attended every prayer meeting I could find.

My spirit was like a dry sponge, opening to a whole

new world and soaking up every drop of spiritual water it could find. Over a period of time I began to see a change. I wasn't quite as cold and hard and aloof with people. I was learning to love myself a little bit more.

I read in Scripture, "'In your anger do not sin...'" (Eph 4:26). I realized there were healthy ways to express negative emotions that I had buried for many years. One of the ways was through tongues. Deep anger with its unknown roots has since poured out from me through this gift of the Spirit.

One gift of healing the Lord gave me was a little product called a "Free Hug Coupon." Inspired by one of my friends, I designed the first version: a simple card that said, "Free Hug Coupon—good for a minimum of one hug from any cooperating human. A hug improves anyone's appearance." I included a loose translation of Romans 16:16, "Greet one another with a holy hug." These coupons captured the attention of the public and multiplied like rabbits. Today they are printed in eighteen languages and are available free of charge to anyone who requests them. Isn't that an example of the mercy of God at work? He called me out of my isolation by giving me hug coupons to design and give to others. I have heard countless stories of how the Lord has used this simple gift to bring healing to others.

In times of enormous stress in my personal life the Lord would remind me of a Scripture that was to become my foundation verse: "... I have set before you life and death... choose life..." (Dt 30:19). On several occasions of deep distress the Lord told me, "Linda, choose life."

Sometimes I would say, "Lord, I just don't know how to do it." He would say, "Your job is to choose. My job is to empower your choice." So I would say (with little faith), "Okay, I choose life, whatever that means." In just a short while God's strength would begin to pour into me.

GOD'S FATHERLY LOVE

When God says, "I will be a Father to you..." (2 Cor 6:18), he means that he will exercise a fatherly role in all areas of my life. God will transform my stubbornness into a tenacity in following him. He will transform my introversion into a gift of enjoyment of solitude in him. He will bring me into balance and transform negative traits into assets.

As my heavenly Father, God will infuse into me an emotional strength and courage to open and blossom. He will instill in me a sense of worth and acceptance, helping me to know how much I am valued, worthwhile, and unconditionally loved in the depths of my soul. God will pour his warm, healing, fatherly love into the roots of my anger, insecurity, loneliness, and low self-esteem. My heavenly Father won't exploit me or do anything to suppress my creativity, my femininity, my energy for living.

As my Father, God has shown me the goodness in my natural father. One of the ways he did this was by sending a man across my path who knew Dad when I was a child. The man had love and respect for my dad in his eyes when he said, "Charlie Vander Ploeg was a master craftsman with a reputation as an honorable business-man."

Another time I was told a story about my father's compassion and love. When a little girl had fallen over a waterfall, Dad wanted to risk his life by going down the falls to rescue her. Others stopped him because he couldn't have made it with the missing fingers on one hand. My heavenly Father showed me many things about Dad that were honorable and good.

God also gave me the grace and compassion to look beyond my father's sins to see the unhealed, hurting man inside. One Thanksgiving Mom told me a wild story about Dad when he was seventy and recently retired. It seems when they were living in Oroville, California, he started regularly visiting a nudist colony. He became involved with a loose, sensual woman and ran away to Mexico with her.

Mom and Dad cried special, God-given tears together for days before he left, as she prayerfully watched him pack his pickup truck with supplies for the journey. "I just have to do this," he explained tearfully. My mother was filled with compassion as she watched him drive away. He seemed like an old man going off to die alone.

The Lord spoke audibly to Mom in her office one day about two months after he left. He asked, "Do you really want a marriage?" Her "Yes, Lord," set things in motion to bring Dad home and restore their marriage. The Lord showed her 1 Corinthians 13:1: "If I speak in the tongues of men and of angels, but have not love, I am only a resounding gong or a clanging cymbal." God impressed on her that love was more important than anything she could do in life without her husband.

My mother shared with me once that a man of God in San Jose named Br. Malone had warned her against marrying Dad. He had said that if she married him she wouldn't serve the Lord. Sometimes Mom would reflect upon all the lost years filled with unproductivity. Then the Lord would recall for her Romans 8:28: "... in all things God works for the good of those who love him, who have been called according to his purpose."

Shortly after she said "Yes, Lord," my dad's pickup truck was broadsided and turned over. For some reason, he landed in a Guadalajara jail. As he sat in the cell with time to reflect, his values inexplicably changed. He couldn't get home fast enough. Mom was there, waiting with the forgiveness that only the Lord can give.

Sometimes we do things that are wrong because we have to or because there is a drive or because we are afraid we will miss out on a life experience if we don't do it. Jesus tells us, "I am here to be what you need. Let me fill that need." Without his grace in our lives, who is to say we wouldn't do some foolish and hurtful things too?

God is my Father. Because of that fact I can let go of my embarrassment about the actions of my earthly father. I can let go of my fear of poverty, rooted in memories of living in cheap trailer parks in dusty towns—and even remember some of the nice places in which we lived. Mom says that I portray Dad as less than he was. She reminded me that he hurt too.

In his work my father was a success, not a failure, Mom emphasized. It was a grace that he was not money hungry, but that rather beneath the rough carpenter's clothes was a sensitive and caring man. She reminded me that his rejection of God probably stemmed from his father, who came home to his first wife and children in South Dakota one day to find everyone dead from a flu epidemic. As a child of a subsequent marriage, Dad probably carried his father's bitter memories. We cannot and must not judge.

God is my Father. All that he is and all that he has belongs to me as an inheritance. All his resources are mine. I don't have to struggle to gain approval or wrestle for position. I am who I am, the daughter of the King of Kings. "I pray... you may know the hope to which he has called you, the riches of his glorious inheritance in the saints" (Eph 1:18-19). I can go forth in security and be a life-giving presence to others, because God is my Father.

Somewhere along the line I began to realize that my problem with men and my inability to bond with a husband especially was related to my father. It became increasingly apparent that something was not right in our relationship. His hands bothered me. One day when I saw him holding my young niece I felt uneasy inside, but couldn't explain why.

I asked Mother one time, "Did Daddy do anything to me when I was a child? Did he touch me in a way that was wrong?" She responded, "I don't think so. But I've been uncomfortable whenever I have seen him holding a child's hand too forcefully." I continued to believe that in some way my inability to bond with a husband was related to my father, but the difficulties were so deeply rooted I could only leave them in the hands of my heavenly father.

CHOOSING LIFE

In September 1984, I was diagnosed with breast cancer and entered the hospital for a mastectomy. During that stay I was ministered to by Mary, a gifted, multi-talented woman who was blinded and scarred in an auto accident and then widowed a few months later. Her wonderful courage gave me the strength to press on.

We need to get that courage from each other at times. We need to draw near to courageous people and let their courage rub off onto us. We need to be with people who are filled with faith and let their faith strengthen us. We need to be around people who are saying yes to the Lord and make room for that yes to take root in us.

The Lord still had some work to do in me in the area of saying yes. On my last evening in the hospital I met a man named Terry. In the three days that we shared an adjoining bath, I was constantly annoyed with him. I would find spills on the floor and things strewn around. The mess made me angry. On my last evening when I was preparing to go to sleep I heard the Lord say, "I want you to go in and pray for that man."

I responded petulantly, "I'm annoyed with him, Lord. I don't want to pray. I don't know him, and I don't want to go in there. Why don't you send someone to pray for me instead?" The Lord wouldn't let me sleep and I tossed and turned restlessly. Then he spoke again, a little more firmly this time. "I want you to go in and pray for him."

Sighing, I put on my robe and slippers and went to his door. He was a good-looking black man in his thirties with a bandage over his eyes. I tiptoed into his room and leaned over his bed. "The Lord sent me to pray for you," I whispered awkwardly. Terry began to cry. "Today I gave my life to the Lord and today I was told that I would never see again. You have no idea how much your coming in here means to me."

When I returned to my room I fell to my knees in deep repentance. I said, "Lord, I am so sorry. Please forgive me. I don't ever want to resist your voice again." I had been feeling sorry for myself about my unknown future. Several of my friends had died following a mastectomy because the cancer had raced uncontrolled throughout their bodies.

After I went home, I bought a world map and pinned it to the wall of my bedroom. I prayed, "Lord, I know you have a lot of things you want to do with me and I don't believe this is the end. I want every purpose that you have for my life to be fulfilled. I choose life, Lord." I would study the map and say, "Lord, give me a love for your world. Teach me how to love the unlovable and reach the unreachable. I want my life to have impact in the kingdom of God. I want to travel, I want to write, I want to speak to your people. I submit my life to you daily. Melt me, mold me, fill me, use me. I give it all to you."

One day when I was out walking and praying with a friend, I had a sudden bold image of a long row of golden doors opening, one after another. When I shared this with my mother she reminded me of the prophecy of the golden path. New doors were clearly opening.

In the spring following my surgery, I began assisting Fr. Robert DeGrandis with his writing. This work was life-giving for me, especially in the midst of my painful family circumstances. The depth of mental illness in my family was overwhelming and known only to a handful of people. The few friends that knew the nightmare of those years also knew the incredible grace of God that upheld me in desperate times. Immersing myself in working on the manuscripts was the healthiest thing I could have been doing at that time.

It was to Jesus and the Holy Spirit that I first became open. It wasn't until later, when the Blessed Mother became involved in my healing, that I would really begin to know the fatherhood of God. My first experience of the Blessed Mother was through a powerful vision in which she appeared and draped her blue cloak around my shoulders. "I will always take care of you," she promised.

During a time of praise at a prayer meeting, Mary spoke to me again: "I'm changing your nature." I saw the Holy Spirit flowing through her nature into my nature, bringing the little girl to life again. In the time to come I was to discover a new softness and gentleness in my nature. The cutting edge to my personality was beginning to melt away.

Not long after that vision I was working on Fr. De-Grandis' book, *Intergenerational Healing*. The Blessed Mother used that opportunity to take me through a life-changing healing. As I began each section of the book, I felt impelled to pray the rosary and to ask Mary to take my request for guidance on the writing to my heavenly Father. Each time I followed that procedure I would receive understanding about the changes to be made in the manuscript.

After about two months and dozens of rosaries, the Blessed Mother asked, "Do you know why I have been doing it this way?" I said, "No." She said, "I've been bonding you with your heavenly Father. You couldn't relate to him because of your poor relationship with your earthly father. Now you can go to him directly." I began to experience a new openness and freedom to relate to God as my Father.

In the fall of 1987, when I was assisting with the book, *Resting in the Spirit,* the situation at home came to a crisis. I was critically ill with a ruptured disk in my back and facing surgery. One day I was lying on my back in desperate pain. The Blessed Mother suddenly swept into the room in a powerful vision, gathered me up in her arms, and took me to the throne room of God.

I found myself stretched out on a golden lounge chair in front of my heavenly Father. There was a sense of personages all around the room, and everything was gold. God reached over and pulled a thorn out of my lower back and handed it to a cherubim on his left, who threw it far away, as far as the east is from the west.

Then my heavenly Father took me by the hand and led me to a door. When he opened the door I saw a long, long, long line of men—most of whom seemed to be dressed in black. God then said, "This is the team I have prepared to help you on the next stage of your journey." After the vision I had a great sense of security, knowing that whatever was around the corner, God had everything worked out. The fact that he also chose men to help me was very healing.

Later on a friend took me to a deliverance conference. I was on a mat on the floor of the seminar with a ruptured disk. A man walked over and said, "The Lord has given me a prophecy for you. May I give it to you?" When I nodded, he said, "It is in song, as follows: 'As the earth covers the mountain, and the water covers the sea, so by the power of my Holy Spirit, I raise you up to be a witness for me.'" The significance of the mountain and sea imagery associated with my childhood in the mountains of the California coast could not have been known by this man. He continued, "I want you to memorize this song and sing it to yourself, night and day."

In the days to come I did as he had said, singing this song in my room at night and in the morning when I awoke. I sang it when I crawled out of my home, unable to walk, and into a friend's home, following a traumatic circumstance at home. I sang it in an ambulance following an automobile accident and on the gurney on the way to the operating room for spinal surgery. I sang it in the recovery room and in the home of friends who cared for me following surgery.

Nine months after surgery I sang it to a crowd of ten thousand people in a stadium in Manila, the Philippines, where I was a part of a nondenominational teaching team.

"LORD, YOU DO IT"

On various occasions over the years, Fr. DeGrandis has commented, "Linda, there is a lot of anger in you toward men." I knew it was there, deeply rooted. I prayed for the Lord to reveal those areas, knowing that the roots were connected to my father, but not knowing how to deal with it. Sometimes I would just throw up my hands and say, "Lord, you do it." That's when the most healing comes—when I invite him in and get out of the way.

One day I shared the horror of the train accident with the late Fr. Joe Diebels, S.J., of San Francisco, California. He took me through a visualization where I pictured Jesus with the mutilated bodies in the dry grass. Just like the dry bones in Ezekiel, the children's broken bodies came to life. When I saw the five children standing around Jesus alive and well, I felt deep peace in my heart. A spirit of trauma left me shortly after that healing session. I have discovered through the years that evil spirits are able to deepen their work in wounded areas of my life especially through traumas.

Incidentally, Bill and I met once more, twenty-five years after our experience on the train. Two middle-aged, gray-haired people, we sat in a coffee shop and reflected on our youthful life as a married couple and the effect of the train tragedy. Bill told me that the man in Atlanta, Georgia, proved not to be his father after all. He never did find his real father. When Bill asked me why I ran away and left him, it was hard to remember. Forgiveness flowed freely.

On another occasion the Lord healed a childhood trauma related to my father. One evening after prayer when I was resting in the Spirit I received a repeat of an image that had haunted me since I was eight years old. At the time Dad's leg was crushed in the logging accident, a family friend named Jimmy Siria had carried him to the car to drive him down the mountain to the hospital in Monterey. When I came home from school I saw the imprint, in blood, of Dad's hand on the back of Jimmy's shirt.

Over the years that image would return, with all its traumatic associations. Thirty-five years later, as I lay there resting in the Spirit, I again saw the image. This time, however, Jesus walked into the picture. He placed his own nail-scarred hand over the bloody imprint and held it there for a moment. When Jesus removed his hand, the imprint was gone. Still resting in God's presence, I became aware that all the pain in the memory was also gone. In its place was a deep, peaceful awareness that the Lord had sovereignly walked back through the years and into the trauma, placing his own imprint on the back of Jimmy's shirt.

When I was in my late forties one of the people the Lord used to bring healing to me was a Jewish psychiatrist, Dr. Joseph Silverman. For two and a half years I spent an hour a week with this beautiful, morally upright, gentle, priestly man. Those were golden hours that I will always cherish. His depth of sensitivity and care of the human psyche was exquisite. Dr. Joe helped me to review the painful years and sort out the wheat from the chaff. With his help, I became stronger and able to make difficult personal decisions.

Because of his example, I also learned how to relate to men, especially priests, in a prayer room environment. After one occasion in which I prayed for a number of priests in a retreat setting, I returned to the psychiatrist and said, "Dr. Joe, I knew how to treat those priests on the retreat. I knew what to do. I knew how to be gentle and sensitive and caring with them. I knew how to listen. Do you know why?"

He smiled and asked, "Why?" I looked deeply into his eyes and said, reverently, "It's because of the way you have treated me all these months—your deep respect for who I am, your sensitivity, your caring, your deep wisdom about people. I learned it from you, Dr. Joe. Thank you." When he said, "You're welcome," we just sat and smiled at each other. The satisfaction for both of us was beyond words.

As I write this I am humbled by the realization that God also used Dr. Joe to father me. Often at points in our lives God will send a father figure or mother figure to fill the gaps left by our natural parents. I thank God for allowing Dr. Joe to model some important aspects of fathering for me.

During the period of time that I was seeing Dr. Joe, my father became very ill and almost died. Paralyzed and near death from a stroke, Dad cried out for help. One week previously my sister had a dream in which she led him to the Lord. That dream was fulfilled as she knelt beside Dad's bed and led him in a prayer of repentance and commitment to Jesus.

Then we all stood back and watched the Holy Spirit heal him. First Dad could move, then sit up, then stand, then walk with a walker, then with a cane, then without aid. His gradual healing was wonderful to watch. After that time everything we asked God to do for him was accomplished quickly and easily.

SET FREE

For five more years the Holy Spirit ministered to my father, gently helping him to be ready to go home. In that time a deep love was released between Dad and Mom. For years, starting after her new birth at age nineteen, my mother would cry out to the Lord, "Teach me how to love. I don't know how to love. Teach me." When she eventually stood at the grave of her husband of fifty-three years, Mom could finally say, "Thank you, Lord. I am learning how to love because of you."

Every time I would make the 500-mile trip from my home in Sunnyvale, California, to my parents' home in

Escondido, I would pray for the Lord to remove the walls in my relationship with Dad. Once I said, "Dad, I just came here to tell you I love you." He would smile and nod, and that would be the extent of my communication with my brain-damaged father for the weekend.

Another time I sat with both my parents at the kitchen table and asked Dad if he would be willing to forgive those who had hurt him. Mom helped bring people to mind and he would smile and nod and say, "Sure, I forgive." Yet for the most part there was no significant breakthrough. It didn't seem to go beneath the surface, yet God used every opening, however small.

Once I even asked Dad to pray for the healing of my headache, thinking that would help open things up. I said, "Dad, would you please put your hand on my head and ask Jesus to take away my headache?" He reached over and put his rough, carpenter's hand with its missing fingers on my head and said, carelessly, "Jesus, take away my headache." He didn't even say the words right, but my headache left. For years I would want to cry whenever I would see a man pray. I had never known my father to kneel or to pray. This was the only time in my life that he laid hands on me in prayer.

In August 1988 I went to see my father for what would be the last time. My sister who is a registered nurse was caring for him in her home. Shortly after I arrived Dad went into a coma. Because there was still unfinished business between us, I began to grieve. It was too late. I would never break down those barriers.

On the last day that I saw him alive, I sat beside the bed of my eighty-five-year-old father with my hand on his chest, praying softly in tongues. The death rattle in his throat told me that time was running out.

What happened as I sat there will live forever in my heart. Have you ever heard a person speak, spirit to spirit? It's hard to explain, but Dad spoke two words that were as clear as the noonday sun. Still in a coma, he said to me, "I'M SORRY!!!!!" The words shot out like bullets from a high powered rifle, yet another person in the room would not have heard a whisper.

Tears began to stream down my cheeks. I knew instantly what it was all about. These words were an apology from father to daughter that came from the depths of his soul, inspired by heaven. He was apologizing for sexually abusing me as a very small girl. How did I know? In that kind of intimacy, you simply know. I whispered, "I forgive you, Daddy." My heart bathed him in love. My father and I had completed our unfinished business.

This final act of forgiveness occurred on the weekend of the Southern California Renewal Convention at the Anaheim Convention Center where Fr. Robert DeGrandis was a featured speaker. Kissing my unconscious father on the forehead and hugging my mother and sister goodbye, I drove to the conference. I wondered why I was leaving his deathbed, yet felt urged to go.

As I mentioned at the beginning of my testimony, I didn't hear a word spoken by any of the speakers that weekend. Not one word spoken over the microphone was meant for me. All during the weekend, I found myself sitting behind the young couple with their tiny daughter. Through my awed appreciation of the blissful love between father and daughter, God was bringing healing to my wounded spirit.

When the priests were leaving in the closing procession at the last Mass of the conference, I went over to the couple and said, "Excuse me, but I've been watching you all weekend." They smiled and waited for me to explain. I turned to the father. "You and your daughter relate to each other with such love, such an open display of affection. That's the way I related to my father when I was her age. You can't know how healing this is for me, because my father is dying right now."

The couple put their arms around me and prayed. When I returned to Escondido, I learned that my father had died quietly that very afternoon, at ten minutes to three—on Mom's birthday.

Two years later at the same regional conference, Fr. DeGrandis asked me to give a brief testimony in his workshop entitled "From Bitterness to Joy." I stood at the microphone and told about the healing with my father on his deathbed and the experience with the couple. Here I was speaking to about three thousand people in that same arena. My voice broke as I glanced at the area where the couple had been sitting two years previously.

Later that day I was standing somewhere in the midst of thousands of people when a couple walked up to me with their four-year-old daughter. The man said simply, "We're the couple." I looked into his eyes and began to cry, a new wave of healing flooding my soul. "We were in the arena," he said, "and heard your story." Fred and Becky Ferguson of Los Angeles, and their little girl, Annie, were God's chosen instruments of healing in my relationship with my father. The healing came so unexpectedly, so simply, so powerfully.

Who would have ever believed that the Holy Spirit would have taken me away from my dying father's bedside, into an arena with thousands of people, to watch a father and daughter loving each other? Who would have thought that the Holy Spirit would have used that encounter to give me back the lost little girl in my heart? Who would have believed that such a powerful work would be accomplished with such simplicity? Who would have believed that the same couple would be in the arena two years later to hear my story?

And who would have believed that sharing this experience in the arena would have prompted so many women to approach me later that weekend with their own secret stories? Who would have believed that so many women are just like me? One said to me with tears in her eyes, "You mean you could really say to him, 'I forgive?' I still can't forgive my father."

I have forgiven my father and I am a different person today because of that grace. Since the healing with Dad I've discovered that I'm not afraid of men anymore. I'm not closed off inside. I can open my spirit and interact more freely now. Jesus loves me, this I know. In that knowledge I am set free.

I am embarrassed by my three marriage failures. Yet I know that I could not have had a close, warm, solid relationship with a husband until I was healed enough to bond with a man. So I forgive myself, accept my heavenly Father's healing love, and get on with my life. "And so we know and rely on the love God has for us. God is love. Whoever lives in love lives in God, and God in him" (1 Jn 4:16).

❖❖❖

Highlights of Linda's Story

- She is baptized in the Holy Spirit.
- She learns about the sufficiency of God.
- She receives the gift of tongues.
- She opens up to friendships and Christian community.
- She learns the healing power of Scripture.
- She spends hours in Scripture, spiritual reading, and seminars.
- She regularly attends charismatic prayer meetings.
- She begins to love herself.
- She learns about God's fatherly love.
- The Holy Spirit gives her a new picture of her father.
- She discovers that all of the resources of God are available to her.
- She realizes that she is a daughter of the King of Kings.
- She begins to reach out to others.
- She repents of times that she had resisted the leading of the Holy Spirit.

- She begins assisting Fr. DeGrandis in writing books on Christian healing.
- She begins to appreciate and turn to the Blessed Virgin Mary as an intercessor.
- She goes through a process of bonding with her heavenly Father.
- The Holy Spirit gives her a picture of a secure future.
- She receives a prophetic vision of the Lord's plan for her life.
- The Holy Spirit sovereignly heals traumatic memories from the past.
- The Holy Spirit works through a Jewish psychiatrist to bring healing related to family mental illness.
- The Holy Spirit works through that same man as a father figure to fill some of the gaps left by her father.
- Her father asks forgiveness for childhood abuse.
- Forgiveness flows between Linda and her father.
- The Holy Spirit completes the unfinished business between Linda and her father.
- The Holy Spirit places in front of Linda an openly affectionate father-and-daughter relationship to give her a picture of her early relationship with her father.
- The Holy Spirit prompts her to talk to a man and his wife who have a good relationship with their little girl.
- The Holy Spirit prompts Fr. DeGrandis to have Linda tell her story at a convention.
- The Holy Spirit brings Linda together with the couple and their daughter again at a later convention.

- As Linda reaches out to tell her story, many women receive healing from their own secret pain.
- Linda is not afraid of men anymore.

Prayer

Heavenly Father, thank you for the golden path you call each of us to walk. Thank you for all the twists and turns of the journey. Thank you for your wonderful promise in Romans 8 to work everything out for the good, no matter how unredeemable the circumstances may appear to be.

I pray now for each person who has been touched in some way by my story. Send your Spirit into each memory that stirred. Touch, heal, and make whole. Thank you, Father.

I pray now for women who have been unable to look deeply into men's eyes because of hurts they have received. I pray for women who have been unable to open their spirits to men or who feel uncomfortable in a man's presence. I pray for those who remember abuses in graphic detail, and those who simply know that something is wrong but can't identify the source of the pain. I pray for the hurt little girl who made an inner vow never to love again, never to open up to a man, never to be intimate, never to bond with a man. Lord, touch and heal her.

Heavenly Father, help them to forgive the wrong done to them. If they are unable to bond with you because of hurts with their earthly fathers, or father figures, please build a bridge. Mother Mary, please come and help with that bridge. Thank you, Lord.

I pray now for men who have betrayed the trust of women. Give them the grace to forgive themselves and the ability to change. Please go to the roots of the motivation to harm and heal the root cause. Lord, touch, heal, and make whole.

I pray now for both the abused and the abuser. Heavenly Father, pour your grace into the desolation, bitterness, and anger. Let each feel loved in the roots of their being. Let them know that in you they are more than conquerors. Give them a picture of the future and hope you have planned for them. Give them emotional strength and the courage to grow and change. Help them to let go of self-rejection and all self-destructive tendencies.

Help those who have been wounded to love and forgive and reach out to others in healing ways. Help them to enter into warm, open, and healthy relationships. Help them to grow and change, to explore new possibilities and expand their horizons. Help them to know that they are worthwhile, always.

I pray now for the children of broken families, who somehow get mixed up in their parents' and stepparents' problems. Lord, touch them in a special way. Help them to feel secure and able to open up to new relationships. Thank you, Lord, for letting them know they are precious and loved. Thank you for letting them know that it is not their fault. Set them free, Lord Jesus, to grow into happy, healthy adulthood.

Thank you, heavenly Father, for transforming your

people into the beautiful men and women you created them to be. Lord, please nurture in their hearts an awareness of the height and depth and wonder of your love. Fill the gap between the love they received and the love they needed. Walk through the years with them and bathe each painful circumstance in your healing love.

Heavenly Father, most of all, bring them into a healed relationship with you. Help them to surrender to Jesus, the source of all healing. In the name of the Father and the Son and the Holy Spirit. Amen.

Afterword

WHAT IS THE COMMON THREAD in these five stories? What can we learn from them and apply to our own lives? They all manifest the transforming grace of God in various ways. They all remind us of the power of prayer. Each person recognized the importance of surrendering to Jesus as Lord. Each encountered a merciful, grace-filled love that became a driving force in his or her life.

Forgiveness is a thread in the fabric of each story. The people in these stories learned that releasing bitterness, resentment, and unforgiveness was a necessary choice. They recognized that forgiveness is a decision—an act of the will, not a feeling. They learned that it is a work of the Holy Spirit. Once a woman asked me why Catholic churches have the crucifix over the altar. After praying about that, I felt the Lord was saying that as he has forgiven us, his death is a call to us to forgive one another.

In fact, we have to die to ourselves and let Jesus enter in order to forgive. "I have been crucified with Christ and I no longer live, but Christ lives in me. The life I live in the body, I live by faith in the Son of God, who loved me and gave himself for me (Gal 2:20). When Mary Ann, Brendan, Sr. Eileen, Fr. Joe, and Linda responded to God's action and forgave, their hearts opened to receive an even greater flow of God's grace. Let's ask the Lord for a fresh grace of forgiveness.

Praise is another thread that runs through each of the stories. Throughout Scripture God is very insistent about praise. When we praise God we are acknowledging his supremacy and authority in our lives. Through praise we are stating that we are weak and he is strong. We are taking our attention off ourselves and our problems and putting it on God. Such a perspective is always healing. The very sacrifice of praise—working at it when we don't feel like it—draws us into the presence of the Lord. Praise opens us to a healthy mental attitude and increases our capacity to grow in love and holiness.

Reflect on the atmosphere of praise that pervades the stories—not necessarily explicitly stated, yet clearly implied. Through my years in the healing ministry, I have discovered that people who go high into praise and deep into forgiveness become very open to God's healing grace. Let us become people of praise! "But you are a chosen people, a royal priesthood, a holy nation, a people belonging to God, that you may declare the praises of him who called you out of darkness into his wonderful light" (1 Pt 2:9).

A growing trust in the Lord is reflected in the lives of each of these five people. Fr. Vincent Lawler encouraged Fr. Joe to trust, stating that the Lord would help him as he placed his trust in him, one day at a time. That is certainly a message of importance for all of us. We don't need to have a supply of trust to last a month at a time; simply trust one day at a time. "Commit your way to the Lord; trust in him and he will do this ..." (Ps 37:5).

THE PARTICULAR MESSAGE OF EACH STORY

The Holy Spirit is working powerfully, outwardly and inwardly, in each of the lives of these five people. Let's look at one particular aspect of each story that might be something we can learn from and apply in our own lives.

Mary Ann. Consider Mary Ann's background. So many thousands of people are afflicted with mental illness that it has become a leading crisis in the world today. Most of us know at least one mentally ill person. Mary Ann was the worst case the nurse on the retreat had ever seen, yet the Lord took that "worst case" into his arms— through the arms of the community—and set her free. Nothing is beyond reach of his free gift of grace. If his people will only pray they will learn that God is love and his nature is to give gifts. Remember the prayers of Mary Ann's mother? Who are the "pray-ers" in your family?

Our loving heavenly Father has many gifts for us, even the healing of mental illness. So often he reaches out to give us gifts, but our hands are closed and we are not able to receive. Let us be aware of his desire to give gifts to us, be attentive to his movements of grace, and open ourselves to receive everything he offers. "Thanks be to God for his indescribable gift!" (2 Cor 9:15).

Another aspect of grace is affirmation. Psychologists agree that most Americans suffer from low self-esteem. One therapist says that after twenty-five years of working with the mentally ill, she believes that all degenerative illness is due to self-hatred. A strong statement, but I feel that some people may subconsciously contribute to their own sickness out of a deep need to punish themselves. They feel they are evil, shameful, and deserve to be punished.

Brendan. Another dimension of God's grace is that it brings us to repentance, to turn away from hurtful and harmful things, and to turn to the Lord. In the testimony of Brendan Walsh, we see a person running headlong into destruction. The turning point was his repentance. I am convinced that Brendan's wife was praying for him. Grace comes as a gift, but usually through the prayers of another person. Again we see how very important prayer is.

In his story, Brendan said, "The desire to go to confession overwhelmed me. I just knew I had to confess my sins. I expected fiery judgment as I laid out my life before the priest, but what I received instead was the compassion of Christ. When I left I felt a lightness and peace I cannot describe. I knew I was forgiven. If that were all I would receive that day, it would have been enough. For the first time in my life I felt clean inside."

When God's grace comes it always brings an urgency of repentance. Repentance and reconciliation give new energy for life, which is evident in Brendan's commitment to be reconciled with his wife and children. Repentance released energy to ask others for forgiveness, a continuation of God's grace.

Through the grace of repentance we are drawn to stop and consider what we have done with our lives, how we have blocked the flow of love, perhaps through gossip, bitterness, or resentment. Some are called to go deeper and face the darkness of certain personal habits and secret guilt. When we are called to repentance, the Spirit will eventually ask us to bring him the areas of life about which we feel the most ashamed. We hide when we feel guilty. God would have us open and free and loving. Once the darkness is exposed to the light, there is a tremendous release of God's grace and mercy.

In repentance we are dealing with an attitude of mind, a choice. "You were taught, with regard to your former way of life, to put off your old self, which is being corrupted by its deceitful desires; to be made new in the attitude of your minds; and to put on the new self, created to be like God in true righteousness and holiness" (Eph 4:22-24). We say, "Lord, I turned away from you by my own will. Now, by my will, I turn back to you." We can repent every day, turning away from that which is selfish and toward that which is loving.

Today, Brendan has a powerful ministry of reconciliation. When he talks about his experience, God's grace touches people so deeply that they cry and return to the sacraments, sometimes after thirty years or more. That is powerful and beautiful. Brendan's repentance marked the beginning of transformation in a remarkable life.

How many others have a new world, a new life, a new ministry waiting beyond the door of repentance? How many gifts and graces is the Lord holding for you, waiting for you to take that step? It's a powerful point to ponder.

Sr. Eileen. As I read Sr. Eileen's testimony, I see a tremendous manifestation of God's grace flowing in community life. Being in a religious community myself, I know that members always pray and intercede for one another. My sense is that the prayers of the community were instrumental in the release of God's grace on her behalf.

At Sunday Mass during the prayers of the faithful, the faith community prays for the needs of the world. There is incredible power released as hundreds of people focus their prayer on each intention. I believe that as people become more involved in a shared community life, the power of the Holy Spirit will be more free to work in them. Behind each healing, you will usually find many people praying.

I am always encouraging people to join a Christian community, such as a Bible study, a sharing group, or a charismatic prayer group. Over a period of time the new person will become integrated into the group and begin to experience the healing of spirit, mind, and body that comes as people pray and share together. Such a community will be a primary prayer support during times of difficulty. When people are depressed and unable to talk to the Lord, even a small prayer community can carry them. "Carry each other's burdens, and in this way you will fulfill the law of Christ" (Gal 6:2). If you are not involved in a praying community, I encourage you to consider joining one. A time will probably come when you will need that kind of support.

Another characteristic of grace is that of pure gift. No one can demand grace or claim any right to it. Because the nature of God is love, he longs to give us gifts. "... God is love..." (1 Jn 4:16). That is the most important line in the Bible because it tells us the nature of God. The nature of a tree is to grow into the air and have leaves. The nature of fish is to live in water and swim. The nature of a bird is to fly. The nature of God is to love. A powerful expression of that love is the giving of gifts.

Fr. Joe. In Fr. Joe Whalen's story, I was stopped by his statement: "Mine has been the most unholy life of any person I had ever known." How does one move beyond that deep sense of guilt and self-hatred into a healthy self-love? God's affirming grace would say to that person, "... you are precious... I love you..." (Is 43:4). "... I have loved you with an everlasting love; I have drawn you with loving-kindness. I will build you up again..." (Jer 31:3-4). "There is surely a future hope for you, and your hope will not be cut off" (Prv 23:18).

We know that God can use even our sinfulness—in much the same way that fertilizer is used for a rose garden—if we surrender all the events to him. For though fertilizer is essentially smelly refuse, it can help produce beautiful roses if applied at the right time to the root systems of the rose bushes in a garden. In the same way, when we turn to God in a posture of humility and repentance for our sins, those very sins can be used as God's fertilizer to produce growth in our lives. Such fruit can also encourage others who are snared by the same sin.

Fr. Joe says that he catches a lot of "big fish" by stressing the fifth step of Alcoholics Anonymous, which is admitting to God and another person the nature of the wrong. In other words, he is able to minister to these sick people because he has been there. Fr. Joe knows their struggle and pain and he can speak their language. His greatest liability became his greatest asset. "And we know that in all things God works for the good of those who love him, who have been called according to his purpose" (Rom 8:28).

Fr. Joe was deeply affirmed by a priest who loved and encouraged him through the rough times as Jesus himself would have done. He reflected, "Fr. Henry Vincent Lawler ... was the most loving man I had ever met in my life." That affirming quality was evident when Fr. Lawler said, "Just think, Joseph, how the Lord Jesus is looking down from heaven and smiling as you put your head on the pillow at night. I can just hear him saying, 'Well done, my good and faithful servant. You didn't drink today.'" This humble priest spoke words of life to lift and build up one of God's precious broken creatures.

Everyone needs to hear the Lord say, "'Well done, good and faithful servant...'" (Mt 25:21). We all need to hear our heavenly Father say, as he said to Jesus at the Jordan, "'This is my Son [daughter], whom I love; with him [her] I am well pleased'" (Mt 3:17). This affirming word nourishes our spirits and gives us encouragement to move forward with our lives. Sometimes the Holy Spirit may prompt us to speak such a word of affirmation to a broken person. Fr. Joe needed that affirmation to move forward in his life. Let's be sensitive to that need in others and ask the Lord for this precious gift.

Linda. Finally, we come to Linda's story. What strikes me here is that the grace of God is evangelical, bringing conversion, drawing individuals to himself. When she was five years old Linda was on the swing, singing "Jesus loves me, this I know, for the Bible tells me so..." As an adult, when she turned on the 700 Club on television and fell to her knees crying tears of surrender, we see the evangelical aspects of grace. "For you have been born again, not of perishable seed, but of imperishable, through the living and enduring word of God" (1 Pt 1:23).

God's grace is always evangelical, bringing us to a point of deeper conversion, bringing us to the point where we desire to base our lives on the Word of God. Linda speaks of the period following her baptism in the Holy Spirit as a time in which she spent hours soaking up every teaching and workshop available. She spent hours in prayer and hours feasting on God's Word. Scripture brought life to her, brought her life into perspective and into order. It helped her to understand God's mind and way and truth.

Today, Linda is a person of the Word and a person of deep prayer. Her success in writing (both in helping me with my books and in her own popular prayer booklet,

Miracle Hour) does not come from college courses, but through long periods of time in the presence of the Lord.

As we read Scripture it becomes a part of us. God's mind becomes our mind. His thoughts become our thoughts. The repetition of Scripture goes deep into our hearts and brings change. Linda has shared with me that during times of physical illness she plays a tape of God's promises in Scripture that she has accumulated and recorded on cassette. She plays the tape over and over, hour after hour, until she feels strength overpowering the weakness in her body. Repetition etches Scripture deeply into the soul until it becomes a part of us. As one thinks, so one lives. Mary at Medjugorje has told the children to take one verse a month and meditate on it, pray over it, reflect on it, repeat it, and let it sink into the depths of their hearts.

In the past, Linda was fearful and withdrawn. Today she reaches out to the world with strength and freedom and ease. The Word of God has been foundational in her process of transformation.

I would encourage everyone to spend some time daily in reading Scripture. Ask the Holy Spirit to guide you. "Your word is a lamp to my feet and a light for my path" (Ps 119:105). "'Is not my word like fire,' declares the Lord, 'and like a hammer that breaks a rock in pieces?'" (Jer 23:29). "For the word of God is living and active. Sharper than any double-edged sword, it penetrates even to dividing soul and spirit, joints and marrow; it judges the thoughts and attitudes of the heart" (Heb 4:12).

Through these five testimonies we have seen the powerful working of grace. We have been reminded of the importance of prayer, surrender, forgiveness, praise, and trust. We have seen that grace is a gift. It calls us to repentance. It is affirming. By God's grace we know we are loved. We see that grace works through the power of a faith community united in prayer. We have seen that grace is evangelical, bringing us to immersion in the Word of God.

The stories of Mary Ann, Brendan, Sr. Eileen, Fr. Joe, and Linda are but a few miracles of God's grace, offered to encourage you in your own journey toward healing and wholeness. His transforming grace is working in each of you at this very moment, uniquely and individually.

The Word became flesh and dwelt among us. Jesus is dwelling among us now, communicating his love, healing, peace, and joy. Amen.

❖❖❖

Questions for Group Discussion

ONE
I'm Not Afraid of the Morning Anymore

Mary Ann's healing began when she reached out to help another person.

1. Consider the action of the Holy Spirit in drawing Mary Ann's attention off her own pain and onto the needs of another person. Can you recall instances in your own life where the Holy Spirit has done the same? What changes occurred?

2. The Sacrament of Reconciliation was an avenue of healing in Mary Ann's life. Reflect on the healing power of this sacrament in your own life. Is there a specific instance that comes to mind?

3. What healing occurred in your life when you were baptized in the Holy Spirit?

4. Reflect on your own testimony of the Holy Spirit's action in your life. What are the key turning points?

5. Sometimes the Lord works in our lives in ways that can only be described as "pure gift." Can you recall circumstances or events in your life that are pure gifts from the Lord? In those events, what did you learn about the nature of God?

6. What three elements in Mary Ann's testimony touched you the most? Why?

TWO
Gently Flows the Dawn

Brendan encountered God the Holy Spirit in a sovereign way at his first prayer meeting.

1. Did God ask him to try to repair the past mistakes, or to begin to live differently from that moment forward? Discuss.

2. Does forgiveness somehow change evil to good? Or does forgiveness release us from the past and enable us to live in the present moment of love? Why? Why not?

3. Do you try to forgive with your emotions? What did the Holy Spirit say to Brendan about that?

4. Are you willing to trust the Holy Spirit to do the same for you?

5. When you meet people do you ask the Holy Spirit to enable you to love and accept them just as they are, so the healing love of Jesus can touch them and draw them to his forgiveness and love? Why is this so important?

6. What three aspects of Brendan's story touched you the most? Why?

THREE
That You Too May Have Life

Sr. Eileen's physical problems resulted from the carelessness of a medical professional.

1. Have you ever been unjustly treated in such a way that it negatively affected the course of your life? How did you handle it?

2. Can you recall instances of being deeply misunderstood? How did you respond? If it happened again, would you respond the same way?

3. Sr. Eileen became aware of making judgments against her father. Reflect on any instances of judgment you may have made against a parent. Is there something that needs to be released? Has this affected your relationship with authority figures?

4. What person in your life is the hardest to forgive? Why?

5. What steps can you begin today to bring reconciliation?

6. What are some of the barriers to healing in your life?

7. When you are hurting, can you forget about yourself and enter into a sacrifice of praise? Is there a particular instance that is significant to you? Why?

8. Sr. Eileen expresses great faith in the healing power of the sacraments. Can you recall instances of healing through these graces of the church? Explain.

9. Sr. Eileen spoke of the dangers of occult involvement. Have you renounced any spiritual contamination resulting from occult infiltration? Do you understand the dangers?

10. What three aspects of Sr. Eileen's story touched you the most? Why?

FOUR
Amazing Love

In Fr. Joe's life it took the full power of the Holy Spirit to work out his deliverance from addiction to alcohol, a dysfunctional family life, and a poor self-image.

1. Do you know the first step in A.A.?

2. Fr. Joe made some decisions to change his environment when he a) went to see the priest, b) started to go to A.A. meetings, and c) began to attend a charismatic

prayer meeting. How important is environment in helping an individual choose a new course in life?

3. Have you taken those steps? Are you willing to seek environments that will make it possible for the Holy Spirit to bring full deliverance and healing to your life?

4. The Holy Spirit began to speak to Fr. Joe through the Bible after he had taken the steps to give his life over to the control of the Holy Spirit. Have you asked the Holy Spirit to speak to you through the Bible about God's will for you? Are you willing to trust the Holy Spirit that God can do that for you? Discuss.

5. The Holy Spirit often uses us to minister to people in situations similar to our own. In what way does the Lord especially use you to minister to others? How has he equipped you for this ministry?

6. Consider God's call for your life. Have you responded to the leading of the Holy Spirit about a particular vocation? Have you resisted the Holy Spirit in this area? Why?

7. What is the most significant moment when you heard the Lord speak to you personally? Why was it important?

8. Who has the Lord brought into your life to encourage you? Name the three most important ways this person has helped you.

9. Fr. Joe says, "When a guy gives up something to help another person, he divides his problems and multiplies his success." Is this true for you? Give examples.

10. When nobody else sees our potential, Jesus does. What is he saying to you today about your potential in him?

11. What three elements in Fr. Joe's story touched you the most? Why?

FIVE
Miracles of the Heart

In Linda's life, it took many years of healing, particularly in her relationship with her father, before she was able to fully receive God's fatherly love and believe that she was lovable.

1. The first step in healing is the knowledge that we are loved. What is your deepest experience of the love of God? How did it change you?

2. Have you experienced the fatherly love of God? How did this affect your relationship with your earthly father?

3. What areas of healing are needed in your relationship with your earthly father? Will you allow God to reveal himself to you as father in a deeper way? Comment on any areas of resistance.

4. Have you experienced the death of a parent or close relative? Can you recall a particular action of the Holy Spirit in that loss? Explain.

5. Recall an instance in which Jesus has walked back into an unhealed memory and healed the pain. How has that changed you today?

6. In her movement toward healing, Linda has experienced a deep sense of the presence of the Holy Spirit. Are you sensitive to the action and the voice of the Holy Spirit in your life?

7. What is your most profound experience of the Holy Spirit's action in your life? How did this experience change your life?

8. What changes could you make to become more sensitive to the leading of the Holy Spirit?

9. If you were suddenly told you had a life-threatening illness, what changes would you make in your life?

10. Have you encountered the intercessory ministry of the Blessed Mother? How would you describe her role in your life?

11. Does the Holy Spirit have work to do in you in areas of saying "yes" to him? Ask him to reveal three areas in which he desires you to surrender more deeply.

12. What three aspects of Linda's story touched you the most? Why?